Praise for
The Culture Climb

"*The Culture Climb* is hands down the best book I have read that explains this complexity but does an amazing job of breaking it down and helping the reader to create a structured and results-focused plan. I want to give this book to every business owner and leader I know!"

—**MARY NUTTING,** founder and CEO, CorTalent

"Culture is a messy, complicated, and misinterpreted element of business. Jaime and Chelsey challenge you to think critically and see why culture is at the root of almost every business success or problem. The book provides real-life examples highlighting the impact when culture is ignored. Through their practical Impact Model, shared experiences, and encouragement, Jaime and Chelsey provide expert advice on how to intentionally enhance your culture. Whether you think your culture is great or know there is work to do, this is a must-read for any leader wanting to get his or her organization to the next level."

—**SETH W. PETERSON,** senior vice president,
First National Bank in Sioux Falls

"*The Culture Climb* is a phenomenal book for any company looking to evolve their focus on brand, culture, and people! I specifically found the Impact Model, broken down into very actionable steps, to be extremely impactful. Setting a foundation and building on it is so often missed, and *The Culture Climb* makes it manageable and actionable. I highly recommend this book to all levels of leadership in a company. If you want to impact change that sticks and takes your culture to another level, this is a must-read!"

—**DIONE DEUEL,** director of brand
experience, Hegg Companies

"Love what the book *The Culture Climb* has to say about culture being multi-dimensional. Culture is complicated. Jaime Taets and Chelsey Paulson do a great job sharing cultural truths that dispel the cultural myths that are present in our workplaces. As the book states, it's about 'clarity, alignment, and right-fitting people.' Amen!"

—SHARI ERDMAN, president, Reell
Precision Manufacturing Corporation

"In preparation for a strategic planning leadership meeting focused on aligning my team around the strategic focus of our organization, I applied the questions Jaime and Chelsey suggested in *The Culture Climb* to my communication to the team. This advice from the book allowed me to immediately apply a simple approach that will help with our focus and cultural health over the next year. I am so honored I was asked to preview this book, and now I have an early start on a more successful year! The best gift ever!"

—DAVID MCCOY, president and CEO,
First National Bank and Trust

"*The Culture Climb* is a perfect complement to understanding servant leadership in the workplace. The people first, allowing data to help define your path, and the teams it takes to make it a culture fit for the new generation of employees are all ingredients for success. Success in your people creates a successful organization. Jaime and Chelsey have shown how easy it can be to make an impact!"

—ANDREA BOLIN, chief of staff,
Mille Lacs Corporate Ventures

"*The Culture Climb* is written at just the right level: broad, yet deep enough to have the reader feel proficient and capable to implement the ideas themselves. It outlines the case for investing in culture without resorting to endless abstract studies and statistics. *The Culture Climb* is a must-read for any organization looking to leverage culture as a core element of their competitive strategy."

—TED WHETSTONE, thought partner

"I loved everything about *The Culture Climb*. Jaime and Chelsea hit the challenges head on and explained why a strong culture enables sustained business results. It isn't a 'nice to have' anymore. It's a requirement—making people feel fulfilled, aligned, and motivated about work. The book contains actionable content to help you intentionally create and foster the type of culture you crave. Highly recommend!"

—**MELISSA JOHNSTON,** chief credit
officer, cofounder, EntreBank

"If you think your organization is thriving based on markers such as sales, customer satisfaction, and overall positive quarterly growth, think again. This is the biggest and most inspiring 'aha' that I gained from reading *The Culture Climb: How To Build A Work Culture That Maximizes Your Impact*. As Jaime Taets shares, in the 'People Age,' thriving means so much more. There is so much content and conversation around what it means to build a great culture, but this book opens real opportunities for your people—and your leadership—to have an honest and robust conversation about how they will feel most alive in their roles so that they can maximize their impact.

Everyone wants to feel valued and *valuable* in what they do, and while the metrics used to be around salaries, bonuses, and other dangling carrots, today your culture needs to be rooted in tapping into the very human essence of what makes each individual tick. In *The Culture Climb*, a resounding theme centers on how 'In the People Age, work can and should add meaning to people's lives.' Many employees have left good organizations because they were not feeling a deeper sense of value. Don't let this happen to yours. Now is the time to engage with your people in a deeper dialogue, and you will be inspired by the vision and strategies that Jaime Taets lays out in this book through her 'Impact Model.' She continues to be the go-to resource for leaders and teams who are ready to roll up their sleeves and create a workplace culture that is truly people-first. This book will show you the way!"

—**MIRJANA NOVKOVIC,** cofounder, Speaker Story Bank

The
Culture
Climb

The Culture Climb

HOW TO BUILD A WORK CULTURE
THAT **MAXIMIZES YOUR IMPACT**

JAIME TAETS

with Chelsey Paulson

**FAST
COMPANY**
Press

Fast Company Press
New York, New York
www.fastcompanypress.com

Copyright © 2023 Jaime Taets

This work is being published under the Fast Company Press imprint by an
exclusive arrangement with *Fast Company*. *Fast Company* and the *Fast Company*
logo are registered trademarks of Mansueto Ventures, LLC. The Fast Company
Press logo is a wholly owned trademark of Mansueto Ventures, LLC.

Distributed by Greenleaf Book Group

For ordering information or special discounts for bulk purchases, please contact
Greenleaf Book Group at PO Box 91869, Austin, TX 78709, 512.891.6100.

Design and composition by Greenleaf Book Group
Cover design by Greenleaf Book Group

Publisher's Cataloging-in-Publication data is available.

Print ISBN: 978-1-63908-032-8

eBook ISBN: 978-1-63908-033-5

To offset the number of trees consumed in the printing of our books,
Greenleaf donates a portion of the proceeds from each printing to the Arbor
Day Foundation. Greenleaf Book Group has replaced over
50,000 trees since 2007.

Printed in the United States of America on acid-free paper

23 24 25 26 27 28 29   10 9 8 7 6 5 4 3 2 1

First Edition

I dedicate this book to all leaders who believe that culture is the leaders' choice and who are committed to creating cultures in their organizations that make an impact.

—JAIME TAETS

Acknowledgments

FROM JAIME

I want to start by thanking Chelsey Paulson for all of her work to help bring this book to life. Her stories and real-life examples added so much impact to this message. And to my team at Keystone Group International for their support to help us get this amazing book to the finish line. It takes a village to create something that has impact, and I am grateful for the amazing people who have supported this book with their reviews, content, ideas, and thought leadership.

To our clients: You are the inspiration for this book. Your dedication to moving from good to great is what inspires us to do the work we do. So many of you have endured a lot as you have scaled your businesses, and I am proud that Keystone has been a part of your journey now and into the future. You inspire us to keep fighting the good fight and creating impact that transcends the work we do.

Thank you to my husband, Curt, and my kids, Nora, Graham, Olivia, and Preston, for your support as I embarked on yet again another crazy book journey. Your patience as I spent nights and weekends consumed in creating something that would have impact was so appreciated. I want to be an inspiration to each of you that you have the power to create a ripple effect by choosing to do hard things.

To our book editor Lyz: You have been by my side for two books and many more to come. I appreciate your perspective, your honest approach, and how you seem to pull out the best of what we have and make it sound better than we could have imagined.

To everyone who makes the decision to buy, gift, or loan this book: Thank you. We started this journey because we knew there were people out there who believed in culture and the long-term impact it can have on an organization. The journey of writing this book has helped me dive deeper into my own purpose around creating shifts in perspective and positive change. And it's helped us think deeply about how we serve our clients as they navigate the uncharted waters ahead. All we can hope is that it has as big of an impact on your life and your business as it did on ours. Thank you for the inspiration to do something that creates a true dent in the world.

Contents

Why Culture Is a Mountain You Need to Climb

BY JAIME TAETS

Are you one of the people who wonder why so many business problems keep coming back over and over again, like a Whac-A-Mole game? I am.

For over a decade, I have been the go-to consultant for executive teams hoping to untangle their issues and to improve their businesses—profits, strategies, and services—along the way. After listening to so many executives share their biggest concerns, spending time drilling into those concerns with a more critical (and objective) eye, and observing patterns, I had a realization: **most business problems are actually people problems**.

Yep, at the root of that Q4 sales strategy that people aren't owning or that process that no one is following is not a strategy or process problem, there is a people problem. And not "people" as in "individuals who are failing on the job." I mean "people" as in the dynamics of how people interact each day to accomplish the work that needs to be done.

This realization shifted my thinking, and my business. My colleagues and I came to understand that most business teams are only assessing the business layer, not the people layer, of whatever's happening. To get at the root cause, they need to go deeper with questions that are rooted in culture and people. For example:

- When we hear, "No one is adhering to the documented process and it's causing issues," we ask, "Do you hold people accountable for adhering to the process?"

- To the comment, "Our managers are spending so much time managing issues, they're not getting time to focus on what grows the business," we respond, "Have you implemented a growth plan to ensure managers are empowering their direct reports, not solving problems for them?"

- When a client tells us, "Our business units are so siloed, we can't get them to cross communicate," we ask, "Do you have a consistent and well-communicated set of values that empowers and enables effective exchanges between units?"

You can probably guess the answer we almost always hear back: "No."

In other words, underneath each of these operational challenges is a more human-centered issue that is going unaddressed—meaning the challenges persist and recur month after month, year after year.

The solution to human-centered issues is culture. And culture is all about people. If you want to get your business unstuck, if you want to take it to the next level, you are going to have to address culture.

CULTURE IS HARD

I was ecstatic when I realized that most business problems are linked to culture . . . I've always led with the belief that once you know the source of the problem, you can fix it! Diagnosis is the hardest part.

But then came another realization: my clients were hesitant to go deep on the people and culture problems because it was *hard*. Like, really hard. They clearly wanted to improve things, but they froze when considering all the intertwined pieces that would go into addressing them. It's complicated; they knew that. Trying to tackle culture was like a game of pick-up sticks: touch one stick and others will inevitably be disrupted. Except in the case of culture, it's not clear what all the sticks are, so you don't know *what all* will be disrupted if you touch one stick. That means while our clients certainly *saw* the deeper problems, they avoided the can of worms and ended up resorting to surface-level solutions. They had no idea *how* to fix the people problems. Process problems? Redesign the process. Sales problems? Get customer feedback. People problems? Nerves, silence, and then excuses and slight deflections.

WELCOME TO THE CULTURE MOUNTAIN

Imagine a mountain (yes, we're starting huge . . . they say go big or go home) and you're at the foot of it, which is the base camp. Each morning, you wake up and figure out what it will take to reach your next checkpoint—all while keeping an eye on the final destination: the summit. Of course, you change plans slightly along the way as you learn and experience more, but you keep on making progress. Then, one day, you reach the summit. Finally, you can stand there and take it all in—the views, the work you put into the climb, and the satisfaction of achieving your goal. And then, once you sit there for a while, you realize there's more work to do, but you already know the value of putting in the hard work. You see another mountain over there that looks pretty awesome, and you begin plotting your next trek.

Improving your culture is like that experience. The base camp is where you're at now, and the summit is a stronger version of your organization that is creating more impact. As you make incremental improvements, you will have a clearer sense of what needs more work and what your strengths are, and how to use all that to go from good to great, from now to better than now. Then, when you reach the summit you will start to see the benefits of all the hard work you put into your culture and also start to see beyond, to even more ways to improve your culture to achieve an even better version of your organization. As you can imagine, climbing requires energy, planning, teamwork, attention to detail, hard work, and a commitment to a longer journey. But on the other side of all that is a goal attained and a new view—of your workplace and people—that is fulfilling.

YOUR CLIMBING GUIDE

The inability of most companies to climb the culture mountain on their own is what gave rise to this book. A few years ago, the excuses my clients had for their lack of progress were frustrating the heck out of me. I had to do something. I asked, *How can I help clients understand and examine their work culture more simply? What will it take so that clients can use culture to grow into better businesses and better leaders? How can I use my concrete experience to push leaders past all the theories about culture and into actually doing something about it?*

In answering these questions, I determined that many companies are stagnant or barely growing because they aren't taking a holistic look at *all* the factors that go into a thriving culture. So I ended up inventing the Impact Model, which is my attempt to depict in a simple way all the working pieces that go into developing a strong culture. The first version wasn't perfect, but that didn't matter. It helped me, and my clients, better understand all the factors at play in their business. Having all the components laid out in front of them—like vision, collaboration, and development—gave them a shared language to use when talking about their issues.

Slowly, in meeting after meeting, I saw the effects of the model. HR people were ecstatic to have a collective way to talk about culture with leadership. Leadership teams started to have different conversations about their workplaces.

Once I realized that getting to the deeper people problems helped leaders get unstuck, I was hooked on using the Impact Model and have continued to refine it over the years with help from people who have a lot of HR and culture leadership experience. The current model defines twenty elements, divided between six stepping stones (see Figure 0.1).

FIGURE 0.1: The Impact Model

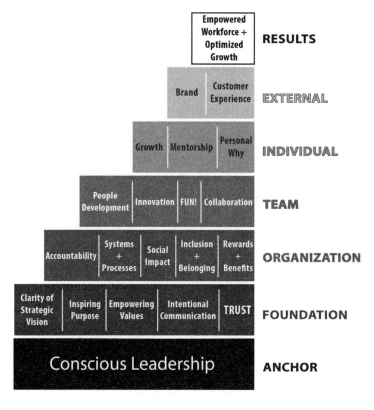

The Impact Model shows how the building blocks of a strong,
positive culture are related to each other.

You'll find much more detail about the model later in the book. The key point I want to make here is that having this model has helped leaders understand the foundation they need to build so their culture change efforts have a positive impact on business results. It defines the checkpoints they need to reach as they climb the culture mountain.

To help you on this journey for your company, the book is divided into three parts:

- **Part I: The Culture Gap** attempts to clear up the confusion about what culture is, how it impacts business performance, and what you must do as a leader to make a positive culture possible in your business.

- **Part II**: **How High-Impact Culture Works** explores all the components of the Impact Model, demonstrates why each is important, and explains how they build off of each other.

- **Part III**: **Taking Your First Next Steps** provides practical steps for starting the hard climb of improving your culture (it is based on tools that you will find on our website).

LET'S START CLIMBING

In our own way, my colleagues and I are making the same climb as what we're asking of our clients—and now, of you. We had to grow so we could serve more teams and wanted to do it the right way. We had to define our own vision and purpose and cultivate a culture that enables us all to help others with their cultures. With all our experiences and opinions, we have created something we're all proud of. We know it will continue to evolve because that's how the business environment evolves, but we believe what we have now can help all organizations and all leaders get a better handle on how they can best grow and evolve, and that's a win.

What we've learned is that it's possible to be a good company without a strong culture, but you will never be a great company without it.

What do I mean by a strong culture? What I want more than anything is for all people to have a work environment that inspires them and allows them to use their strengths daily. We spend too much time there for it to suck. A strong culture is a positive culture: people leave work feeling better than when they came in. Finding small ways to positively influence our environment is something I take to heart. It drives my relationship with clients and is one of my filters for success. I also like to get moving quickly. When we started writing, I said I wanted to be able to provide a book that was easy to follow and understand so people could spend less time reading and more time doing. I think we learn so much as we go. We can research and think all we want, but once we're in there doing the work, that's when we really figure things out.

So, I hope that when you finish this book, you feel better than when you started because you have a little more clarity around the topic of culture, and you know your first next step. It might challenge you or make you realize you have to stretch yourself, but I know on the other side is a path to being a better leader, leading a better organization, and creating more impact.

PART I

The Culture Gap: Why You Don't Get the Results You Expect

Every day, every year, organizations spend time, energy, and money defining ways to get better, maybe even to achieve greatness. They reach for broader market share, develop programs to help more people, find new ways to meet changing customer needs and wants, strategize how to grow, and explore ways to stay relevant. There are a variety of approaches, but we believe there is one clear way to beat out the competition and build the strongest version of your organization possible: culture. And not just any culture, one that's specific to the human needs and organizational needs of your workplace.

The starting point is to understand the complexity of culture and find the right intersection of both the people and the company so you can go from a good organization to one that performs higher, has a richer employee experience, and cultivates a more positive environment—one that will get you the results you want: the revenue, influence, and impact. Laying the foundation for this work is what we talk about in the following chapters.

CHAPTER 1

The Culture Gap at Work

"If you are lucky enough to be someone's employer,
then you have a moral obligation to make sure people
look forward to coming to work in the morning."

—JOHN MACKEY

"Into our ninety-eighth year, we're bigger than we've ever been. We're making more money, our budgets are growing, and we're getting more customers. That is amazing. I want us to celebrate that." Katherine, the CEO of a large manufacturing company, was looking around the table at her leadership team. They all smiled back at her. "But I still feel like there's more potential in the market that we're not capitalizing on." She knew this wasn't what they wanted to hear—they thought the meeting was going to be all about pats on the back given the strong year they had just finished.

"This again?" asked Devon. "I feel like we keep talking about this sense you have that we can get much bigger." He shifted in his chair, rested his elbows on the table, and continued, "It's not that I don't want it, but I guess I'm starting to wonder if your hunch is right. We have the talent we have. The services we offer are fine and are working, and we're seeing some growth. I just don't know what 'better' could even look like without huge changes."

Katherine considered Devon's pushback while also acknowledging what a strong CMO Devon was. He always hit his metrics and he never missed a meeting. His team performed well overall, though they seemed to be somewhat fixed in how they did their work. He was a very different type of leader than she was: he kept his team under tight control whereas she had more of a "hire well and let them do their jobs" philosophy. *We all have our own way*, she thought. *That's not a bad thing. Or maybe it is?*

"I know, I've been banging this drum for a while," said Katherine. "And I will keep beating it; I think it's worth our time to talk it out. I want us each to answer this question: Are we just going to keep going the way we're going, which isn't bad, or do you think there's more we're leaving on the table?"

Sheila, the head of HR, confidently replied, "I think there's more market potential out there." The rest of the team nodded cautiously with various degrees of confidence. Devon glanced around with some disbelief. "Well, since I already showed my cards a bit, I'm going to say no. Obviously that goes against the grain, but I just don't see it."

"Thanks for being honest, Devon. Disagreement isn't necessarily a bad thing. I truly want to hear everyone's thoughts. Given that most of us think there is room for us to grow, I want us to talk about what we believe is holding us back." Katherine saw that her leaders were a bit nervous. Here sat the C-suite team—the COO, SVP of Sales, CMO, CHRO, and the for-now-empty CFO chair—all figuring out how to essentially critique themselves. Whatever was holding them back as an organization was on their shoulders, right?

"I'll start," she continued. "We've gotten really focused on sales over the last few years. Jennifer, as the SVP, you've taken a lot of that on yourself. You've reconfigured some of the processes and spent a considerable amount of time upskilling your team. The results speak for themselves; revenue is up. But our profitability has been nearly constant as the revenue increased. So we're making more sales but not more money."

"Yeah, I've noticed that too," said Jennifer. "We spend a lot of time as a sales team talking about improvement and growth, which makes sense— we're salespeople, we're hungry go-getters. But we don't feel like all the other teams have that same drive. I don't want to blame anyone, but it's just hard to stomach sometimes." Jennifer paused, waiting for any reactions from around the table. She felt a little self-conscious because she didn't want to tattle on the other teams, but she went on, "I have to be honest, there is a lot of drama on the delivery team. We see them constantly tossing problems around and then when someone from our team goes to sort it out to keep things moving, they throw each other under the bus. So yes, I think we are leaving something on the table, but also is this the business that we want to grow? Is it even scalable when we have so many inconsistencies? If we go from $40 million to $60 million, I feel like these issues are just going to balloon. We already don't really want to work closely with that team, and I can't see it getting better with more clients and bigger projects."

Brandon, the COO and head of the delivery teams, appeared a little miffed. He had always espoused that command and control was the best way to lead complex projects. He was productive and smart, though not a real people person. "Your team is always interrupting our work with ideas on how to change things. We just want to put our heads down and get things done! If you're constantly trying to 'grow,' how do we have time to do the work that's already on our plates? When my people work with yours for project handoffs, they comment that everything is so different that they don't know what to expect or how to work with your team. I don't want to sound negative, but it really takes effort for them to flip back and forth between our teams, given the dynamics. And to answer your original question, Katherine, my two cents is that our pay grades are what's holding us back. It's so hard to find good people; when I'm out trying to recruit new people for my team, I get ambivalence that I can only attribute to our somewhat conservative pay philosophy. I think that might also be why our retention is so bad."

"That's fair, Brandon," Jennifer admitted. "I know we've been doing a lot of work without sharing it out, and that might be leading to some internal confusion among our teams."

Sheila cleared her throat. Usually the last to speak up to ensure everyone else got their floor time, she took an HR approach and thought about what she had observed recently. "I have to say, people seem a little unsure about how to contribute after Shawn's departure last year. He was such a strong force around the office, kind of the self-appointed welcome committee, and he often drove up the excitement at our staff meetings. I think when he left, people weren't clear on why or how such a visible contributor is going to be replaced. I know that doesn't explain why we didn't grow much before that, but I noticed a significant change around the office after that. I have a hard time describing it, maybe it's like hesitancy? Or people just seem a little less energetic around the office. CFOs aren't usually such fierce figureheads, and I think we made an assumption that we didn't need to do a lot of messaging or follow-up about him leaving. I think how we managed that left an impression."

Devon chimed in. "I'll just say it again. We have the talent we have, we have the services we have. I just don't think we can do much more with it than what we're doing. We've reconfigured our offerings so many times and yet here we are." He sat back, frustrated that they were spending so much time on this issue that didn't appear to really be an issue. They were fine, they were making money, why did they have to try and find problems?

Katherine took it all in. "Well, there is a lot to unpack here. What I know is that we could keep going on as is, and that would be okay. Or we can aim for more."

BELOW THE SURFACE

Did you notice the one word that *wasn't* mentioned in the discussion Katherine had with her leadership team? Culture. Yep, much of what these executives *didn't* say points to culture. We heard:

- There are inconsistencies in how people across teams behave.

- Leaders are leading their teams using different approaches, and it's confusing people.

- Teams, and maybe even individuals, don't trust each other.

- A recent big change rocked the workplace's energy and it's gone unaddressed.

- They cite pay as a reason they can't recruit people, but they don't actually know that.

- They've tried solving bottom-line problems with top-line strategies, but nothing is changing.

- They keep talking about getting better, but they aren't seeing any major improvements.

- Poor communication around a leadership departure caused instability.

These diverse symptoms are all indicators that cultural issues are operating behind the scene that are preventing people from doing their best work. They are all signs that point to a need for an investment in culture. Katherine and her team may not see it right away. That's not entirely surprising. Oftentimes, leaders can feel some pain or discomfort, suspecting that they have a weak culture. But other times, they might be entirely unaware of how the culture that's sitting right below all the behaviors is affecting their business. Both pain and ignorance are detrimental to you and the culture. And we're not writing that to scare you. It's just that we've seen this over and over: leaders ignoring what we know are major signs of culture gaps because either they don't interpret them as culture gaps or they don't know what to do. So, let's talk about culture.

YOU CAN FEEL CULTURE
EVEN IF YOU CAN'T SEE IT

Culture is not as concrete as some other parts of business, and that's partly what makes it a bit slippery and hard to grasp for business-minded people. In fact, definitions of culture abound:

- In "The Leader's Guide to Corporate Culture," published in the *Harvard Business Review*, the authors wrote, "Culture expresses goals through values and beliefs and guides activity through shared assumptions and group norms."[1]

- In "Culture: 4 keys to why it matters," McKinsey defines culture as "the common set of behaviors and underlying mindsets and beliefs that shape how people work and interact day to day."[2]
- Indeed, a leading job website, defines work culture as "a collection of attitudes, beliefs, and behaviors that make up the regular atmosphere in a work environment."[3]

You have likely read definitions like these and used one like them in your own workplace, or at least in how you think about your work culture. They are all correct, as are the myriad other definitions, because there is no standard definition.

Still, if you want to discuss culture within your organization, it helps to have a definition you can use so you can establish a common vocabulary and understanding. For us, a simple definition of work culture, borrowed from Peter Drucker, the legendary management consultant, is what works: **your culture is the way people think, act, and interact with each other, on teams, and with your customers and partners.** These behaviors are guided by and revolve around a collective mindset defined by your purpose, values, and other agreed-upon ways of being.

For example, suppose Big Food Company, Inc. (fake name, obviously!) has established that they value creativity as a mindset. This means an employee thinks about their work and their contributions with creativity in mind. They look for creative approaches, know they can propose out-of-the-box solutions, and draw on established creative principles, like divergent thinking, as they solve problems. They may generate new product ideas based on the expectation and permission to be creative rather than, say, an expectation to use evidenced-based thinking.

Science has shown us that whatever we think informs our actions. So employees at Big Food Company, Inc. will make decisions, create outputs, structure meetings, and take all the other actions that make up their day with creativity in mind. Perhaps they will create an unorthodox presentation or pitch a client who isn't right in the target market because they know their creative efforts will be accepted and maybe even rewarded. Then, knowing that creativity is a shared belief, individual employees will interact with people at their workplace creatively and allow others to show up that way too. So if someone opts to do that unorthodox presentation, their peers will lean in and embrace the unexpectedness because they also value creative approaches to their collective work. That sense of creativity and all the subsequent behaviors that happen because of that shared belief ultimately create a feeling of what it's like to *be* at that workplace and who you *can be* at that workplace.

How every person thinks, acts, and interacts creates the energy of the place. You know, that feeling you get from a company when you're in their office, when you're using their services, or when you call them up for customer service—you can *feel* their culture when it's positive. And while culture is all about people, it has a huge sphere of influence over your company's reputation, performance, and perception—essentially, your impact.

Oftentimes, we think of work culture as only impacting the environment inside the walls—that's why a kegerator or a ping-pong table are considered "culture"—but culture seeps into every extension of your company and how it shows up. For example:

- How people respect boundaries between work time and home life

- How individuals are supporting or improving customer experiences

- How well processes like onboarding and reporting are understood and adhered to

- How people are rewarded for good work and how people are reprimanded for bad work (e.g., not completing assignments when they say they will or plagiarizing)

- How meeting etiquette is established and enforced

- How people's daily work is being organized and evaluated in relation to overall organizational goals

- How people treat every human that walks into your building (clients, vendors, people who are lost and wandering around the hallway)

- How much employees are supported in developing new skills

HOW CULTURE INFLUENCES BEHAVIOR

You might be wondering how this all syncs together . . . the feelings, thoughts, behaviors, etc. That's a lot of moving parts. Below we've taken three examples from the list we just gave and show how a shared belief, whether explicitly or implicitly communicated by leadership, may influence how individuals behave.

- How people respect boundaries between work and home life
    - Shared cultural belief: working hard is our first responsibility.
    - Thought: I shouldn't leave early or I'll risk losing that promotion.
    - Action: books a meeting with several teammates at four thirty.
    - Interaction: judges a colleague who takes time off to caretake a family member and makes sure their boss knows about the incident.
    - Feeling Competitive (*It's each person for themselves.*)
- How individuals are supporting or improving customer experiences
    - Shared cultural belief: customer happiness is our top priority.
    - Thought: I'm empowered to make things right with customers when something goes wrong.
    - Action: proactively calls a customer that received the wrong order.
    - Interaction: confidently shares the error with the shipping department who are grateful because they are also driven by making things right, no matter who gets the credit.
    - Feeling: empowered (*It feels good to make others feel good!*)
- How well processes like onboarding and reporting are understood and adhered to
    - Shared cultural belief: we each know our own right way.

- ° Thought: departments own their own processes.
- ° Action: redesigns their department's onboarding experience without sharing changes with the HR team.
- ° Interaction: is confused when HR challenges their new documentation and begins to distrust the head of HR who decided to overrule the changes.
- ° Feeling: frustrated (*Am I empowered or am I not?*)

As you can see from the examples, behaviors throughout all levels of a company—individual, team, and organization—create the culture. Organizational behaviors communicate to employees and customers what the company cares about and how authentically they express their culture. If a company says they value people but continually cuts benefits, individuals (internal and external) might start to wonder if leadership actually cares. Teams also have a collective way of behaving that is often dictated by the team culture, which can be slightly different across teams even within the same company. If a company values "community involvement," one team may express that value in volunteer work and another team may express it as fundraising for a chosen not-for-profit. Both teams are living the values, just expressing them differently.

DATA DETOUR

EMPLOYEES BELIEVE CULTURE IMPACTS NEARLY EVERY ASPECT OF THEIR WORK.

The Eagle Hill Consulting Workplace Culture Survey from 2018 found that employees believe workplace culture has a strong impact on their job performance.[4] Here is what employees had to say:

- · 77% said it impacted their ability to do their best work
- · 76% said it impacted their productivity and efficiency
- · 74% said it impacted their ability to best serve customers

continued

- 73% said it impacted their commitment to help achieve company's goals
- 70% said it impacted their commitment to ethical behaviors
- 67% said it impacted their creativity and innovation

If employees *think* culture impacts them, it certainly does: How we think determines how we act. And the Great Resignation only underscored the impact culture has on people leaving or staying at a job.[5]

BEING INTENTIONAL ABOUT CULTURE

Culture is always present, regardless if leaders—or you—are actively and deliberately working on it. There is always a set of behaviors that create the culture of a place or "the way things are." But intentional culture happens when you purposefully shape and inform the thoughts, actions, and interactions that you expect from and reward people for. That doesn't mean everyone behaves exactly the same; it simply means that everyone is clear about the parameters of the collective mindset and what's appropriate, and then finds their own way to express themselves within that.

For better or worse, there's no single way to have a good culture—there are many work cultures that are intentional, and they look and feel all different ways. That's partly why culture work is so difficult. Busy executives want a playbook. They want an off-the-shelf approach that they can plug and play. (Okay, enough clichés.) But spoiler: there is no exact recipe. The way a culture expresses itself at one company won't necessarily even make sense in another company. You have to do the work and define the type of culture you want to create. Just as there are many ways that workplaces can feel bad, unsupportive, confusing, disjointed, and more, there are an equal number of ways they can feel positive, empowering, clear, and meaningful. That's why we call this effort the Culture Climb.

EXPERT TIP:

BE READY FOR THE SKEPTICS

Now, some employees can be skeptics of culture as a path to real business impact. They think it's fluff. They remember the years they put in feeling underappreciated, overlooked, and struggling, and they think that's just how work is. You gotta put in your time. These same skeptics also tend to believe the myth that culture is the feel-good stuff that doesn't impact the "serious" aspects of business like revenue and productivity. Our message to them: we see you, we hear you, and—respectfully—you're wrong. If you have a person like that on your team, we'll help you make the culture case to them. If you happen to be that person, then we promise to change your mind. Or at least make you doubt your beliefs a little more.

CHAPTER 2

Six Truths That Bust Common Culture Myths

*"The best preparation for good work
tomorrow is good work today."*

—ELBERT HUBBARD

When we start talking about culture with teams, peers, and clients, one thing becomes really clear really quickly: there are a lot of myths about what culture is and how it operates at work. These myths take hold and grow because the human brain loves to make up stories. Perhaps you once heard of a company trying to _____ [*fill in the blank*] to improve their culture, and you also heard that it didn't work. Now that thing, whatever it is, is lodged into your mind as something that doesn't work without any context about the thing or the circumstances in which it was tried.

It's a bit like culture Mad Libs. Do you remember those from your childhood road trips? It was a two-person game; one person asked the other to say nouns, verbs, and adjectives based on the blanks in the Mad Lib story. The person saying the words had no context; they simply said random words. In the end, you read back the story with their words and it was always absurd and borderline nonsensical. That was the fun of it! But in real life, the same effect gets us in trouble. We end up with all these ideas of what culture is, or isn't, based on stories we hear, often with context lacking. That mixed bag becomes our truth, even if it's based on myths. And what happens is those myths turn into blockers, excuses for people to not even try to improve their culture. We want to confront some of the myths head-on by sharing six truths about culture.

TRUTH 1: CULTURE IS NOT ANY *ONE* THING

One of the biggest myths people believe is that culture can be pigeonholed by some simple description.

In many companies, for example, culture is the "fun stuff." You know, the foosball table, the suites at sports arenas, and team barbecues. Business is the business stuff, like projects, pitches, and clients, and then culture happens between and around the business. Yes, the fun, or social, elements contribute to the way people develop relationships with their peers, but building relationships can't compensate for a culture that's weak in other ways.

When we talk to clients who aren't initially convinced their culture needs any improvement, we like to ask what they currently do to develop their culture—maybe they're on to something good! But they almost always share a version of, "We installed a kegerator in the break room, created a hangout space where we encourage them to take a break from projects, and offer season tickets for teams to use to celebrate big accomplishments." We ask, "How'd that work?" And we get a response like, "It didn't seem to impact anything, so we just don't think it's worth investing more."

In fact, we had a client come to us to help them after they suffered from the it's-the-fun-stuff misconception. The year before, the company had invested nearly $100,000 in an office renovation with a focus on cool collaboration areas, play elements like a ping-pong table, and other "fun" details that encouraged hangouts. Right after they finished the renovation, their engagement survey scores actually went down. As you can imagine, that was frustrating for the leaders. They spent all this money to make the office space better for people, and employees were *less* engaged? So we went to work using focus groups and small roundtable conversations with the teams to figure out what went wrong. It turns out, their employees were hardworking but also burnt out. The last thing they wanted was to spend more time at work, even if it was playing games. And when they saw the office renovation, it actually negatively impacted them because they knew that all that money that had gone into the office could have been used for giving employees a few extra days off, which is what they truly wanted. The leadership team unfortunately missed the mark entirely by assuming what people wanted rather than asking. Moreover, they also assumed that fostering a good culture was equivalent to fostering playtime at work when really a good culture starts by talking to your people and creating the culture together.

Companies like these are operating within the myth that culture is a single thing and if you try a single thing, it should work. The original statement was that the office renovation "didn't seem to impact anything, so we just don't think it's worth investing more." Our correction is, "It didn't impact *culture because culture includes so much more, so it's not worth investing more effort in only that one piece of culture.*"

Imagine an employee who enjoys hanging out with their coworkers and playing a game of foosball with them every once in a while, yet every day that employee comes to work, and those same coworkers aren't held accountable for the projects and goals the company has set. If that employee is working their butt off to contribute to the bottom line and sees coworkers not taking the same amount of responsibility, the employee won't feel a strong sense of culture. That foosball bonding won't do much to offset the unfairness, or possibly even resentment, they carry, and that hardworking employee will probably jump ship. Because without accountability, it's just a crappy work environment with some intermittent socializing. Who wants that? No matter what "one thing" you think encapsulates culture, it's always more. If you've invested in one way and didn't see results, that doesn't mean culture can't impact your business positively, it just means that one thing didn't impact your culture positively. And because culture is never just one thing, you generally have to focus on a few areas at one time to actually see the impact.

Here's another "one thing" that clients often use to excuse not working on their culture: "We do annual engagement surveys and get positive results." Hear us now: engagement and culture are not the same things. Engagement surveys measure how an individual feels. The respondent is answering questions about themselves: "How do I feel? Do I feel like I am contributing to the company mission? Do I align with the values?" Me, me, me. A culture survey, or a real assessment of your culture, will ask those "me" questions but also ask questions about the collective, like, "How do *we* work together? How do the *teams* interact? Does *leadership* demonstrate accountability?" Culture assessment is about how individuals feel *and* about the greater good: it's me *and* we. Both are important because an individual can feel engaged and yet the culture as a whole can be inconsistent or accidental. The only way to know if the engagement is *a result* of the culture is to also ask bigger questions that place the individual within the context of the whole. Positive engagement is great! Engagement is one of the results of a good culture and can help make your business successful, but again, it alone doesn't equate to culture as a whole.

Culture is not just the social stuff, the surveys, or team building; it's all that *plus* some. Culture is multidimensional, and because it's made up of all those thoughts, actions, and interactions, it's dispersed and can be hard to see. It's the hidden hand described in chapter 1, or maybe an iceberg is a better analogy: there are a few elements like the social stuff and engagement surveys that you can see and easily do. But those are just the elements above the surface, while many other aspects of culture are hidden below, such as how well the company's vision and purpose are understood and expressed, the clarity of core values, and people's ability to live the values. These are dimensions that are more difficult to see, but you can feel them simmering beneath the surface. Individuals feel all the dimensions and express them in various ways nearly every moment at work. Culture weaves its way through *every* thought, action, and interaction that unfolds, and so we have to examine all the dimensions together. This leads us to . . .

TRUTH 2: CULTURE IS COMPLICATED

We're not going to lie: culture is complicated. It's so tempting to think culture is just one thing because, damn, that would make it so much easier to understand. Yet, it should also be a relief to hear that it's complicated because that's why you haven't mastered it already! If it were easy, and it was simply buying enough baseball game tickets, then we'd all have the happiest, highest-performing companies possible. And we don't. So it must be more complex than the "one thing" myth.

As we mentioned above, culture is multidimensional. As mentioned in the preface, our attempt to capture that aspect of culture results in our Impact Model that has twenty building blocks, and we realize that may evolve over time. We might add more or we might take some away because what is meaningful at any given time can be different from previous times. What individuals wanted and needed out of work in 1985 is different from what people in 2010 wanted and needed and what they need and want now or a decade from now.

Culture evolves and so must you. We'll speak more about this concept of evolution (and the patience required) later in this chapter, but what's important to note here is that the multiple dimensions mean there are exponential combinations those dimensions can take. In fact, quantitatively speaking, there are over one million ways to combine twenty things. And, that's assuming each of the twenty things only manifests in a single way—and in the case of culture, that's not true. Qualitatively, mentorship can look so many different ways, so even within each of the twenty building blocks, there is a lot of variation.

The complexity of culture is one reason why there is no standard or "right" way to express any of the culture building blocks. It's just about clarity, alignment, and right-fitting people. We can look to some big brands as inspiration, like Zappos or Netflix, that in their own ways blazed the culture path and showed us what is possible when companies invest in culture. Zappos made headlines with their adaption of holacracy,[1] and Netflix published a deck about their culture in 2009 that transparently shared what made their culture *their* culture.[2] Much has been written about both of these companies, but if you read everything and tried to emulate them with the intention of "creating a great culture," it wouldn't work. Zappos's culture reflects Zappos, no other company. Netflix's culture reflects Netflix. Neither can be transferred to other workplaces.

We think the complexity of culture is why so many books about work culture are often theoretical and vague. They tout things like "consciously collaborate" or "align policies, processes, and procedures," but how individual leaders inside their own organizations *do* this is often ignored. I think we can all agree that if we could align by saying, "We'd like to align," we would be better off. But we need more than that in a practical environment. We need to be able to point to something to align around and then figure out an intentional path to get there.

That's why you have to find *your* culture, and that's the complicated part. Again, we're not trying to scare you. This is where the real opportunity and potential come in for you and your company. You can find *your* way! But it's like therapy. You have to dig into the different parts of your company, carefully assess behaviors and sentiments (including your own), listen to what everyone has to say about your culture and evaluate what you really want it to look and feel like, and then map out changes to try and get there.

TRUTH 3: CULTURE IS NOT ASPIRATIONAL

Before we get too far along here, we have to make a point here: culture is not aspirational. Culture is how people are thinking, acting, and interacting *right now*. You can have aspirations to evolve and grow your culture (you should, in fact), but the vision for where you want to be cannot be confused or mixed up with how things are right now. This is important because we often hear people talk about their work culture more as how they want it to be, not necessarily how it is every day for the people in their organization.

Having a vision for how you want your culture to grow and change is a good thing, but it's risky to confuse the vision with the current reality. We had a client—we'll call them Build Corp—that acquired another, smaller company. As they completed their merger, the leadership team at Build

Corp was really interested in bringing the culture they had created over the years to their newly acquired company and teams. So, they started to roll out their vision and values and other building blocks that introduced their core culture to the new organization. A year or so went by, and even after the rollout, there was something that the smaller company wasn't quite feeling. See, the parent company had a vibrant community involvement aspect to how they worked—their staff volunteered, they actively sponsored events, etc.—so "being a part of the community" was a big part of how they all thought, acted, and interacted at work. But that simply wasn't the case for the newly acquired company. The leadership team at the acquired company thought community involvement sounded well and good, but they just didn't *do* that as part of their day-to-day activities. This gap between what the culture proclaimed to be and what actually happened at the workplace meant that "community involvement" wasn't yet a part of their culture, no matter how much it was written in a handbook or on the intranet. We had to break it to Build Corp that you can't claim aspects of a work culture if it's not evident in the feeling of your workplace and the actual ways people are taking action. You can work on it! But you can't claim it.

TRUTH 4: CULTURE IS EVERYONE'S RESPONSIBILITY

Every single person is responsible for culture. We're going to take a two-step approach to explain this point. First, let's talk about leadership and HR, then we'll open it up to "everyone."

Traditionally, the "people stuff" has been delegated to HR so we often see companies that explicitly or implicitly believe culture also lives in HR's court. Leadership focused on the business, HR focused on the people.[3] But if you divide responsibilities up in that way, intentional culture can't take hold. What it means to be an effective leader has changed from the times when that division made sense (if it ever did, but that's another topic). In the early 1900s, whoever was the most dominant person was the best leader because that attribute was what drove business. Then we moved into the information and intellectual age, and whoever had the most information and the most smarts was the best leader. And now we've moved into the people age, and whoever can best relate to and understand people will be the best leader. If you want to be a good leader in today's business environment, you have to own the people stuff, too. (More about this in chapter 5.)

Okay, now let's broaden this topic a bit. Perhaps you understand why leadership and HR need to come together and make great workplaces for employees, but why does *everyone* get a role in culture? If culture is made up of people's thoughts, actions, and interactions, then one person's inappropriate or inconsiderate actions can impact the feelings about the environment. Think of how dispiriting it can be if someone keeps showing up at meetings underprepared and overconfident, derailing conversations without any consequences. And if they do it routinely or have even more off-culture interactions, then it introduces some issues and even negativity. On the other hand, every person at every company has the opportunity to support, empower, and recognize the people around them every day—to create a positive work culture. Peer-to-peer culture can be as impactful and as positive as top-down culture. Think of how awesome it is when someone at a meeting tells you that you crushed it—it doesn't matter if it's your leader or a peer; you feel great and your day is a little better.

Because culture is everyone's responsibility, every individual will influence the culture. You can't gloss over that one person who is a culture problem but who is also a high performer. You can't hire a new cut-throat, go-for-the-jugular finance director and think it won't impact the benevolent nature of the rest of the team. It will. Every person will contribute something to the collective pot. That fact alone isn't good or bad; it's just a fact.

TRUTH 5: CULTURE IS MEASURABLE

We see leaders eager to invest in new infrastructure, additional sales training, or more social media ads to improve or grow their business before they will invest in culture. On the one hand, we get it: the ROI can be easier to measure on those tactics. But the evidence is there to support the fact that a strong culture enables sustained business results. You can't get to what you're capable of without a strong culture or, if you get there, you can't sustain it. Remember that comparison between the two teams—one with an okay culture and one with a great culture? The great culture team had energy after they got to the end of their project. They were ready for more, maybe even *wanted* more. That, my friends, is a true competitive advantage.

"If we can't touch it, then we can't improve it . . . right?" We've heard variations on this comment from many people, and some of the same people often rely on this "culture is too squishy" as an excuse to not address it, or not to measure it. The reality is you can touch it (not literally, just metaphorically) if you break it down into parts. Of course, it's not like measuring profit, which is a relatively straightforward equation of revenue minus expenses. That's why starting from an understanding that culture is not any one thing is so helpful—it starts to crack open another way of thinking about culture and how it operates. If it is multidimensional, then you start to consider each dimension as a different aspect that you need to measure.

Here is one measurement *about* culture that's been well documented: studies have shown that companies with positive cultures outperform their competitors. For example, the "*Fortune* 100 Best Companies to Work For list shows that it's the companies that employees say are great workplaces that demonstrate stronger financial performance, reduced turnover, and better customer and patient satisfaction than their peers."[4] Organizations are measuring the effects of culture quite reliably now. So there is no reason culture itself can't be measured. Yes, culture is multidimensional so it's hard to quantify. Yes, it's everyone's responsibility so it's hard to make one person accountable for it. But you *can* measure it, and then you can more easily track the value of the investments and see where you should do more or pivot to another strategy. A Catch-22 about investing in culture is that you have to measure it to demonstrate its ROI. This means you have to invest in measuring, getting a baseline, and improving before you can feel the return. It's a bit of a leap of faith, but you won't make any traction or grow in a positive direction if you do nothing.

TRUTH 6: CULTURE REQUIRES PATIENCE AND EVOLUTION

In business, we often want to see improvements quickly. We want results. Now. Maybe even yesterday. So the truth that culture will take time, and will constantly evolve, often makes leaders uncomfortable. An investment is much easier to make if the results come in three months. But what about three years? That might feel like a lifetime, but it's also how long a real, sustainable culture can take to build. Taking time doesn't mean it's not worth doing, and it doesn't mean you don't feel some positive effects early and often on the journey. But it does mean that your big goal—your summit—isn't just around the corner.

So much of our lives—personal development, raising kids, friendships—is like this; it can't be completed one day and then tucked away in a drawer never to be considered again. Quite the opposite. We work at each facet every day, a little at a time, and all that work adds up to something meaningful. It's like the perspective author Simon Sinek shared in his book: business and life is an infinite game.[5] It's never done; there's always more to do. It takes patience and persistence to play the long game, but it's also the most fulfilling approach.

At times, we hear people write off culture as if it's a fad. How culture expresses itself may have trends, but culture itself is rooted in timeless human needs. We believe that fundamentally, baby boomers and millennials (or any generation) have similar core values.

Take trust, one of our core building blocks, as an example. Pensions were how companies built trust with employees in earlier generations. The exchange was simple: employees gave their time, companies gave them pay into retirement. That agreement reinforced the trust between the organization and the individual. But now, millennials have witnessed the recession of 2008, the collapse of Lehman Brothers, and the mortgage crisis. Not surprisingly, they don't automatically trust that big businesses will always do what they say they will do. They know that something catastrophic can go wrong between now and retirement.

There is a generation of workers who are making companies *prove* that they care about the individuals *now*. Not in forty years. And that desire for trust *now*, not later, has led to conscious capitalism. Another example of enduring values but changing expression is family benefits: boomers wanted a pension/401(k)/insurance; Gen X wanted maternity and paternity leave time; millennials want pet insurance. These are all expressions of human values and expectations that companies should recognize to support employees' home life and care about their family needs, in whatever way employees define "family." These are the factors that can and will change over the course of time, but trust is an outcome that must be maintained.

Culture will continue to look different at your organization. It's not ad hoc or a one-time thing. You have to be able to be constantly growing and iterating on the next, better version because there are always new conditions within which your culture is operating. A new leader starts at the company, a new product launches, a competitor merges with a bigger competitor. All these things—the economy, turnover, leaders, current events—change the here and now, which impacts people, which impacts culture. To sustain the strong foundation and positive culture you (hopefully) want, you will have to adapt as factors around your culture change. There is always something to reflect on and to evolve.

WELCOME TO THE PEOPLE AGE

Devoting time, attention, and resources to culture isn't only about making people feel good generally (another myth). It's about making people feel fulfilled, aligned, and motivated *about work*—how they show up, why they show up, and what they can contribute. That's optimal. Humans want to care about what they do; it's our instinct, but many workplaces simply aren't creating the conditions people need and want to contribute their best stuff—like a clear vision and direction or a strong path for developing and growing within teams. That means effort and intelligence are left on the table.

In the People Age (we made that up, but you can borrow it), you will spend time on people. And people are complex; change will require patience. The workforce environment is shifting enormously right now, and really has been for the last ten years or so. Whether you're competing against other organizations or against younger generations' interest in going out on their own, one of the primary efforts that retain people or bring new people to your company is the culture. Fostering a positive culture can help you evolve into what people want and need so they can contribute fully in the workplace.

CHAPTER 3

How Culture Connects to Results: The Impact Model

"Culture isn't just one aspect of the game, it is the game."

—LOU GERSTNER

You probably already know on some level that culture is important. This isn't your first rodeo, and we're not the first people to say culture matters. But still, something drew you to the idea of being more explicit about how to influence culture. And we have a hunch about what it is: most leaders today know they're supposed to care about culture, but they don't know exactly what culture *is* in action, and because of that, they don't know how to do it well, or at all. So instead, they do a bunch of ad hoc changes. They delegate culture to HR. They write some values, stick them on a wall, and hope culture grows from them. They focus on the fun aspects of culture and hope people feel good. No shame if you've done any, or all, of these ideas. But unfortunately, none of that adds up to an intentional culture that propels your business to do better. And you probably know this, too.

Regardless of how you define culture and what you have (or have not) tried to shape it, culture is most effective and powerful when you are able to fully understand all its parts and operationalize them. To do that, you need more than a definition, you need to understand the specific elements that make it up. By breaking it into parts, you can begin to understand and tinker with them, and only then to construct an intentional culture that gets your organization the lift it needs to go to the next level.

The question therefore remains: How can you effectively and positively influence those thoughts, actions, and interactions? The answer is by cultivating a culture that unites the factors that both businesses need to succeed and people need to thrive. That is how you turn culture into rocket fuel and is what we talk about in this chapter.

THE HEART AND MIND OF BUSINESS

Organizations assess numerous factors to survive or hopefully thrive at every moment.

Some of the factors reflect the **business needs**: Are the company and the services relevant? Does the company have the talent and assets it needs to grow? What is happening externally that may threaten the corporation's industry, and how does it stay ahead with a purpose that is unique and future ready? How will the organization remain viable and competitive in the market? Why does it exist, and how will it differentiate? How will the business develop the skills and operations it needs to keep pace with growth? Fundamentally, every organization needs to clearly answer these questions for itself and for its employees. That information provides the big picture that can help individuals inside the organization know where it's going and hopefully compel them to get on board.

These business needs are matched by the **human needs** of the people working in the organization. Employees are also assessing personal factors to determine if they're in the right role at the right company: Do I believe in what we're doing? Are my basic needs met, and am I able to contribute to my best ability? Am I proud of the work I'm doing? Do I see a future here? The answers to these questions inform how individuals feel about their experience at the organization, how they take action, and how they understand themselves (and their effort) within the whole.

A culture that both successfully articulates and shares the core business needs *and* successfully addresses and satisfies employees' human needs can create a truly activated workforce. People have what they need and want, and they clearly understand what the organization needs and wants. That combination creates an empowered culture of people who can and do make a significant impact on business outcomes (Figure 3.1).

FIGURE 3.1. The basis for high-impact culture

A great business culture takes into account both the "head" (Business Needs) and "heart" (Human Needs).

When you approach culture this way and use culture to drive your growth, you will ask different questions about your business and your people. If you don't meet a quarterly business goal, you will examine your culture and ask, "What could be improved here so that we can achieve it next quarter?" There is always a reason you succeed or miss the mark, and you can often find that reason buried somewhere in your culture.

Providing leaders with the specificity they need to be able to diagnose cultural challenges and identify what can be changed to improve both business and human outcomes is what led us to develop the Impact Model.

THE IMPACT MODEL:
HOW TO INFLUENCE CULTURE

Showing people a diagram with a brain, a heart, and a strong arm is useful conceptually but doesn't help people understand what exactly it is they can do to change their culture so they can get the business results they want. That's why we developed our Impact Model that you can see in the preface (repeated in Figure 3.2). It's a tool we use to work with leaders to point out concrete actions they can take to tackle culture.

FIGURE 3.2. The Impact Model

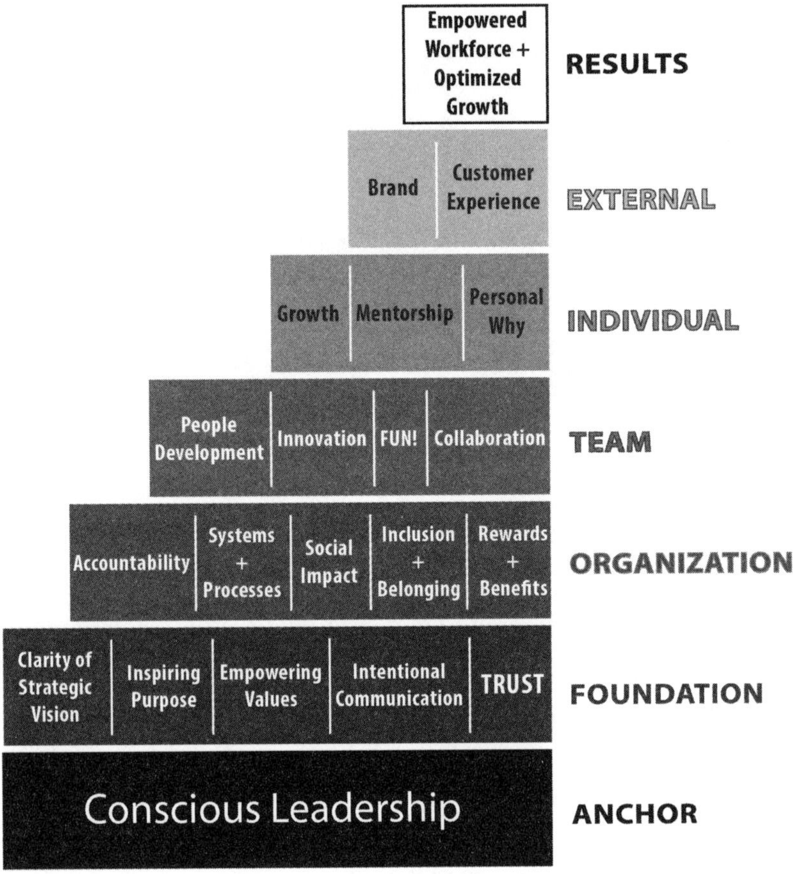

The Impact Model's building blocks are arranged in a sequential order to create the conditions for a positive culture and performance. Each level of the model is designed to fuel and fulfill an empowered workforce so that the organization can grow and evolve into the best version of itself.

- The fundamental element is the conscious leader who provides strength to the system, always mobilizing people into action. The foundational building blocks give people within the organization the framework to be successful—together they provide both the head (knowledge) and heart (motivation) for an organization to succeed.

- The organizational level digs a little deeper into operations to ensure the entire organization is connected, supported, and moves together.

- The team-level blocks represent best practices to keep people on teams working effectively together.

- Then the individual level amplifies what people need to succeed on a personal level.

- Finally, the external blocks name important factors that are affected by and continuously affect our work cultures.

These building blocks, when they're implemented successfully, represent a framework for a positive culture that will lead to better results. They each provide what people need to do great work and what great organizations need to prosper.

All of part II is devoted to exploring the model and understanding what all the components mean and the synergy between individual blocks. For now, we want to emphasize that each level creates the strength, structure, and support for the subsequent level, but the blocks directly influence the others, too. They bounce, interplay, relate, support, push, and advance others. And if one block is weak or not executed well, it can bump, decrease, or deflate the strength of other building blocks or of the entire foundation. They are powerful together and individually. This goes back to culture being complex. You can break the blocks apart and see each one as a singular aspect of culture, but you also have to know that they will always intertwine and influence each other.

When you finally operate in that magical intersection of business needs with human needs, when you can look carefully and honestly at all these critical aspects of your organization, you will start to truly experience the power of culture with an empowered workforce and optimized growth. That's how the Impact Model can help your organization. Let's examine some ways you can apply the model.

DIGGING UP THE ROOTS OF YOUR ISSUES

You can use the dimensions of culture depicted in the Impact Model to diagnose issues—by considering each one in relation to the goal, you ask better questions. Instead of assuming people (or yourself) have to work harder or faster, a culture-based inquiry can get to a deeper behavioral understanding. Maybe it's looking carefully at your people development strategy to determine if people have the right skills to contribute effectively to the goal you missed. Perhaps it's examining your communication plan to understand whether people truly grasp your vision and understand their role in achieving it. The reality is that growth rarely happens effectively or sustainably with a "better, faster" approach, and using culture to fine-tune how you're working will lead to better results than simply doing more.

We have a saying at Keystone: **stop mowing dandelions**. Let us explain. If you have a beautiful grassy lawn in the spring and suddenly dandelions spring up everywhere, you get frustrated. But there are a few ways to get rid of the annoying dandelions in your yard. Week after week you can cruise over them with your lawn mower, which makes your yard look better for a few days. But after those few days, you start to see their little heads poke up again and the prickly leaves get fuller. And when it's time to mow the lawn again, those dandelions are suddenly as big as they were the week before. I'm sure you see where we're going with this . . . mowing dandelions doesn't get rid of them. It might even make them worse—the seeds take flight and spread, and then you have more and more until you're overrun.

So what's the other option? You have to get down there, roll up your sleeves, and dig the dandelions out by their roots. One by one, you grab them and deal with them once and for all. The same is true of organizational (and people) problems. If you try to just deal with what you see on the surface, without examining what's going on below, you won't fix the problems; you will simply delay the issues. Even if digging deep takes a little longer than the mowing approach, our advice is to opt for short-term discomfort over long-term dysfunction.

Delaying can fester into frustration and impatience because your team will end up talking about the same issues over and over. This saps energy. But when you dig, you start to get new data and have new conversations; you may even start to see matters differently. New perspectives and new inputs are crucial to effective problem-solving. And when you start solving problems, you get unstuck and tackle the next concern that will make your organization better. Not every solution will be perfect, but developing the ability to examine and probe deeper is a great business practice.

We had a client who mowed the lawn several times before realizing the futility of their initial approach. The leadership team was rolling out metrics for their call center—goals for call times, response times, number of calls closed per day, etc. When they introduced the plan to the teams the first time, they were met with resistance and frustration. The leadership team considered the situation and determined that given all the complaints, the metrics must be the wrong ones. So, they went back to the drawing board and reconfigured the expected time, the close rate, and tweaked the other numbers with the hopes that the department employees would feel better about the plan. They rolled out the redrafted metrics and were met with similar resistance. The leadership genuinely wanted the team to be on board, so they started thinking about how to make people feel more supported. They figured training would help ensure everyone was equipped to take on the tasks and draw on the appropriate skills to achieve the metrics. Yet, even after the training sessions, the call center team was frustrated. That is when leaders realized they were not digging deep enough to truly understand the problem.

Once they started examining more closely the components of their efforts, they started to gain traction. It wasn't *what* they were rolling out that was causing the friction, it was *how*. It went back to how leaders were communicating and how they designed this new system. Their command-and-control approach to the initiative didn't align with the culture that was present in their workplace, and employees responded to that. While this is a micro example, it's representative of what can happen both to projects and to work culture overall when the underlying causes of frustrations and problems are not examined and assessed from a behavioral angle.

As we've stated several times before, most business problems are rooted in culture and people problems. You can tweak, change, or reinvent parts of your business all you want to solve issues, but if you don't weed out any deeper behavioral or cultural insufficiencies, nothing much will change. In the case above, the root cause of the frustration was based on communication and how it felt to people, not the actual metrics themselves. When you have all the parts of culture laid out in front of you, you can use them as a road map to guide your problem-solving. Each part gives you the language and perspective to examine how strong and effective each one is. Addressing issues from a culture perspective and examining all the people stuff helps you get to the root of problems because it forces you to ask different questions. *Could it be that we haven't been clear about our vision and that's why our sales teams are still pursuing disjointed projects? Could it be that our reward programs are actually disincentivizing people? Could our multistep customer feedback process be impacting our team negatively?* If you don't start asking the deeper people questions as habitually as you ask the business ones, you simply won't be solving the real problems.

In the call center example, the leadership team eventually did consider how they were working and realized their own actions created adverse effects (ouch). But once they moved through that and adopted a more intentional communication plan, finding ways to collaboratively create the metrics, their culture (and their leadership) was stronger for it. They fostered trust, the leadership flexed new skills that paid off, and they could finally get moving on measuring meaningful data about the organization's effectiveness.

EXPERT TIP:

IF YOU DON'T "HAVE TIME" TO SPEND ON CULTURE, YOU PROBABLY NEED IT MORE

Do you ever hear yourself saying, "There isn't time to work on culture" or "We have other priorities"? If culture isn't already a priority or something you're consciously spending time on, that's a sign that said culture probably isn't as strong as you think it is. Culture needs to be cultivated; it is not self-sustaining. Culture always exists within an organization, so if you're not spending energy on it, it's growing and changing organically. And if you think about a garden, you know organic growth can go many directions . . . You might get some perennials that pop back up each year, or, in other cases, weeds could take over your flower beds. Time spent up front will be time saved later.

A HIGH-IMPACT CULTURE OPTIMIZES GROWTH

The other result of the Impact Model is optimized growth. It's common knowledge that every organization must be in growth mode most of the time—adapting, evolving, or improving to stay relevant and afloat. While every organization has moments where they pause and hold steady, you can only do that for so long or you'll get left behind. And that's never been truer than today. Technology has increased the pace of change and the need for organizations to stay up to date. Expectations and needs are evolving quicker and quicker, and the business requirement is that now we must all be in a perpetual state of adaptation. As individuals, we are used to this—we are constantly learning and growing. It might be in small ways, like when new traffic patterns created in our neighborhood reroute us. It might be in larger, more significant ways like going back to school to expand our skills. Whatever it is, we can each say that we know more and different things than we did ten, five, or even one year ago (especially given the COVID-19 pandemic). This should be true of your organization, too. As businessman Andy Grove noted, "You have no choice but to operate in a world shaped by globalization and the information revolution. There are two options: adapt or die."

The Impact Model provides a road map for this required, and inevitable, growth. The building blocks create the path to a successful business and shape practices and conditions to both review and renew your path forward. The building blocks are timeless and constant. Your purpose may evolve, but the fact that you need one and need to use it to drive business decisions will not change. The same is true of organizational vision, belonging, and each of the other building blocks. How each is expressed will change, but the need for each of them at work in your organization will not. They are optimizers, if you will, to help you decode and structure your growth. If you're consistently attentive to the basic needs represented in the model, you will help your organization become better in the ways that make sense for your market, your people, and your purpose.

WHAT LEVERS CAN YOU PULL?

Taking an objective look at your company and culture is hard. We know. We're all so close to what's going on inside our business, we're so personally invested, and we often feel under pressure to move fast. But what can seem like the quick and easy path now can lead to an ongoing game of Whac-A-Mole that ultimately is inefficient. Your organization can't prosper if it's trying to solve the same problems over and over again. When you become aware of all the moving pieces that create a culture, you can better diagnose where your current culture is holding you back and what you can change to improve results. You gain awareness, buy-in, and momentum as you strive to become a great organization.

CHAPTER 4

Culture as Fuel: Why the Climb Is Worth It

W hen your culture is cultivated around empowering people, your overall employee experience will improve, which in turn helps you grow. When employees feel a high sense of trust and psychological safety, and have leaders who encourage growth and development, who view change and failing as positives and the way to innovate, then they will feel empowered to act autonomously while keeping the best interest of the company and the customers in mind. When these optimal conditions are met—employees will *want* to help their leader and the organization reach their goals. This is key. In the *Harvard Business Review* article, "Why the Millions We Spend on Employee Engagement Buy Us So Little," author and work futurist Jacob Morgan examined companies who invest in overall employee experience, not just engagement. He defined experience as "creating a place where people want, not just need, to work each day."[1] It sounds like culture, right? He found that companies who invested in experience were included:

- 28 times as often among Fast Company's Most Innovative Companies,

- 11.5 times as often in Glassdoor's Best Places to Work,

- 2.1 times as often in *Forbes*'s list of the World's Most Innovative Companies,

- 4.4 times as often in LinkedIn's list of North America's Most In-Demand Employers,

- Twice as often in the American Customer Satisfaction Index.[2]

He also found, "Compared with other companies, the experiential organizations had more than four times the average profit and more than two times the average revenue. They were also almost 25 percent smaller, which suggests higher levels of productivity and innovation." He concluded, "Looking at the data, it's clear that there is a significant return to organizations that focus on employee experience over the long term, not just engagement in the here and now."[3] The goal is to create a workplace that provides an overall positive experience in an individual's life—that's the start to a great workplace culture.

Let's take a closer look at how paying attention to culture will pay off for your organization.

THE LINK BETWEEN CULTURE → PROFITS

Most business leaders want healthy profits. That makes obvious sense: the reality of business is that every company needs to make money to exist, so profits are simply mandatory. Without them, everyone would be out of a job. So, if profits are mandatory, it's a leader's job to figure out the best way to make them. Leaders are doing this all day long—seeking and assessing the various levers they can pull to make their businesses as strong and successful as they can be. But along the way, they are often focused on the bottom-line numbers and then working backward. What if you inverted your attention? If you invest your time and energy in your culture, the profits will come.

While money isn't everything, it often makes the biggest impression when teams are deciding on or re-upping a commitment to culture. So how do culture and organizational performance relate? Study after study has shown the undeniable correlation between a strong culture and strong financial results. Comparative cumulative stock market returns among the publicly held *Fortune* 100 Best Companies to Work For® are nearly 3x greater than the market average.[4] In 2018, FTSE Russell found that companies on the *Fortune* 100 Best Companies to Work For list returned 11.66% annually from 1998 through the end of 2016, nearly 5% more than the equivalent returns for the benchmark US all-cap Russell 3000® Index (6.72%) and US large-cap Russell 1000® Index (6.68%). They also found the thirteen public companies that have been on the *Fortune* list every year since the beginning have scored a cumulative return of 495%, compared to 170% for the Russell 3000 and 156% for the S&P 500.[5] In the white-paper "Return on Culture: Proving the Connection between Culture and Profit," Grant Thornton and Oxford Economics found that companies with extremely healthy cultures are 1.5x more likely to report average revenue growth over 15% for the past three years, and public companies with extremely healthy cultures are nearly 2.5x more likely to report significant stock price increases over the past year.[6]

PREPARING FOR THE FUTURE: WHY CULTURE CHANGE IS IMPERATIVE

There are thousands of articles proclaiming the value of great work cultures, and yes, you can get all the outcomes the *Harvard Business Review* article say will happen, but *why your company*? Why should *your leadership team* do something that may require you to face uncomfortable realities about your company? Why should you do something *now* when there are inevitably other things competing for your time, investment, and attention?

We're going to answer that question with more questions (you're welcome; it's one of our superpowers). Has your marketing plan stayed the same over the years? Do you use the exact same sales process from when you started the business? How about technology—are you using the same computer, server, or data processing tools you did ten years ago? Unless you're a CEO at a new start-up, our guess is that aspects of your marketing, sales, and technology have changed over time. Sometimes those changes happened out of necessity; some may have occurred with hopes for optimization. More likely, and more commonly, they change because the conditions around you change and you must adapt. In all aspects of business, we have to adjust to the times or we will become obsolete—this is true for culture, too. If you want to keep making an impact—however you define that—you have to continuously invest in your culture the same way you invest in other parts of your company. Here are a few other reasons we think it's worth your effort.

BETTER SUSTAINABILITY, IMPROVED RESILIENCY

When you create a positive culture, you also create a more sustainable organization. Turnover happens: you will, at some point, leave your role, and other leaders you work with will also leave theirs. It's just the nature of business. What you don't want, amid those changes, is a complete implosion of the business itself. You see this quite a bit when founders leave the companies they started. Without realizing it, the culture centered around the founder—their behaviors were modeled but were not necessarily documented and established as values. Their decisions and actions conveyed a "way of working," but not one that was ever intentionally shared throughout the organization. Because of this, without them, the rest of the operation wanders aimlessly a bit until either they go under or they bring on another strong leader who can shape things up into a new iteration of the business. And while we might not all be thinking about it daily, creating a culture that transcends you, or any individual leader, and establishes a strong foundation that outlasts you is remarkable and generous.

A positive culture can also contribute to an organization that withstands all the happenings we know are inevitable: crisis, purposeful business pivots, external pressures, and more. When organizations are stressed or pressure tested, culture is often what determines their success or failure. A strong culture can help teams weather storms, like the recent COVID-19 pandemic. Crises don't create the cracks or weaknesses in your culture; they simply expose and potentially exacerbate them. When external factors like recessions, inflation, or social catastrophes occur, your culture may have to adapt or evolve, and that's best done when you already have a strong foundation upon which you can draw.

DATA DETOUR

EMPLOYEES WITH A GREAT EXPERIENCE AT WORK ARE 25X MORE LIKELY TO STAY FOR A LONG TIME.

One study found that 4% of millennials who do not experience a great workplace don't plan a long-term future at their companies, while 90% of millennials who feel they are at a great workplace want to stay there for a long time. In other words, a great workplace makes a 25x improvement when it comes to retention. For Gen Xers, the numbers were 6% and 95% (17x improvement), and for baby boomers, the numbers were 14% and 97% (a 7x improvement).[7] People *want to* stay at workplaces that feel great, and if they want to stay, they likely also want to contribute.

INCREASING THE VALUE OF YOUR BIGGEST ASSET

People determine your impact. Without also folding a deep understanding of people into your business efforts, your investments won't create the same impact. It's common knowledge that people are the biggest expense at any organization. Payroll, benefits, training, etc. add up. You can continue to view this all as an expense, or you can view it as an investment. Instead of trying to minimize the expense, why not maximize the asset? Let's consider our personal lives for a moment. For many people, their house is often their biggest expense and biggest asset, analogous to people at a company. And we know that to retain the house's value, they have to invest. Sometimes work helps maintain the home's value, like replacing the roof or fixing a plumbing leak. But other times, the home's value increases by adding improvements, like building an awesome new deck in place of old sod. Good companies maintain their culture; great ones improve their culture. Culture is an investment in people to ensure they remain your biggest asset.

There are two important themes that support our work on culture improvements with leaders: engagement and empowerment. A 2021 Gallup poll found that 36% of the workforce feels engaged with their work. That number has been basically the same for years (with the exception of 2020 when the number was all over the place, for what are pretty obvious reasons). While we do not believe engagement alone tells you everything you need to know about your culture, it's pretty safe to assume that the 64% of people who are *not* engaged are not contributing their best work, and their leaders are not getting optimal results. Perhaps a few rock stars can be disengaged and still do great work, but if that's the case, imagine what they could do if they were actually engaged! Now, in this case capacity isn't about getting more and more out of your employees, like a productivity challenge. It's about leveraging people's strengths and tapping into the skills and passions that may not be obvious in their role. It's about empowering people to think beyond their job description and more deeply into what they have to offer as a person, a whole person, not just their job title. When you mine your peers and staff for more, for what they care about, and create a culture in which stepping up and extending help or proactively solving problems is expected, you get more from people, and they want to give you more in return—which will benefit the organization. Gallup research has shown that "strengths-based cultures see 8% higher revenue per employee compared with the average."[8]

Imagine you and your team are working toward an enormous goal. Not only will accomplishing the goal mean great things financially, but it will also set you apart in your market. You have to push and ask a lot from everyone in the company on your way to hitting it; it's an all-hands-on-deck effort. In that moment, while your sights are on the big goal, there is only one vehicle that will get you there: your culture. And culture is the only thing that will help you consistently achieve new goals and sustain growth time after time. A weak culture cannot hold up over time to the evolutionary imperative companies face today. Your organization simply can't become the best it can be without an intentional culture that addresses the core needs of the humans involved and the business needs of an ever-changing industry. And when you do this, you embark on a journey to become great.

DATA DETOUR

CULTURE IS THE MAIN REASON PEOPLE CONSIDER LEAVING THEIR ROLES.

The 2017 *What People Want Report* by Hays, a US recruitment company, found that culture is the main reason people would consider leaving their current role, with 34% overall listing it as the main motivator and 47% of active job seekers saying it is the reason they are leaving their current role.[9] We hear from leaders that pay is why people leave, but the report tells us otherwise. How people *feel* is a bigger contributor to the career decisions they make.

A HIGH-IMPACT CULTURE FOSTERS ENGAGEMENT

Empowered individuals know how they can contribute, feel ownership of their roles, and encourage others to contribute fully. They have the autonomy to make decisions and the guideposts to make those decisions in alignment with the organization. How you create your culture, and the specific culture you establish, will empower people to act in specific ways. By developing a strong innovation culture, a company can signal that experimentation and learning are more valuable than always doing things the same way. By prioritizing social impact, a company can connect staff members and deepen roots within their communities—extending the ways individuals see themselves within their sphere of influence.

Empowered people give more of themselves because they want to, not because it's expected. In fact, empowerment fuels engagement because an empowered employee intrinsically *wants* to contribute. They're motivated to stay engaged because they feel more responsibility and ownership of the organizational outcomes. Perhaps your purpose and values resonate with your employees' personal purposes and values. Or maybe the benefits and rewards help employees achieve personal goals. Whatever is inspiring them to lean in to the organization, they are indeed leaning in. In *The Relationship Between Engagement at Work and Organizational Outcomes 2020 Q12® Meta-Analysis: 10th Edition*, Gallup found that across companies, business/work units scoring in the top half on employee engagement more than double their odds of success compared with those in the bottom half. Those at the ninety-ninth percentile have nearly five times the success rate of those at the first percentile.[10] Similarly, Gallup's ninth edition of the same title found that median differences between companies that scored in the top quartile of engagement compared to those that scored in the lowest quartile had a

- 10% increase in customer ratings,
- 21% increase in profitability,
- 20% increase in sales production,
- 17% increase in production records,
- 24–59% reduction in turnover, and
- 41% reduction in absenteeism.[11]

You might be thinking, "But hey, you said previously that engagement surveys were not culture. Now you're saying engagement is one of the outcomes we want?" Engagement and engagement surveys are just skimming the surface of how you can understand and measure work culture and the employee experience. Yes, you want people to be engaged, and you also want to put that engagement into action—that's when the culture starts to actually take form. So, engagement is just the start. Typical engagement surveys aren't enough to give you a full understanding of your culture but do give you an understanding of the level of satisfaction and health of the relationship with work, especially when delivered periodically. Pulse surveys provide a more active trend line to engagement, helping you see how your teams are doing over time rather than in a moment in time. What you're looking for in the statistics shared above is sustained engagement or the ability to maintain a high level of engagement by employees throughout their years of service. This is done through a well-crafted employee experience that takes a holistic view of how the workplace interacts with an employee and vice versa.

DO YOU WANT A GOOD CULTURE OR A GREAT CULTURE?

The difference between a good culture and a great culture will determine the true level of success an organization achieves. Imagine two teams at two different companies, one with good culture and one with great culture. They each have the same goal: to finish a big project for their newest clients in a tight timeline. They both start working hard and, lo and behold, they each accomplish the goal. They finished! But how they work along the way and how they feel at the end are very different.

The good team is exhausted and burnt out. But what's worse is that they trust each other less than when they started because of how they collaborated (or didn't) over the course of the project, and half the team feels like they got the short end of the stick because they were relegated to doing rote work, not the more challenging strategic thinking that the project lead did.

Let's contrast that with the great team. They are also exhausted and a little burnt out, but they are psyched to take on the next project. Their organizational purpose fueled them to find innovative ways to tackle the project, and they all worked together to come up with a new process that was hard to perfect at first, but once they nailed it, it really sped up their work. They each took on roles and tasks according to their strengths, and so while it was a hard project, they felt motivated by the challenge. In the end, they were having fun approaching the complexity and they learned a lot that they wanted to share with the rest of the organization.

From the outside, these two teams did the same thing, but on the inside, the people on the teams felt very different, and the ways their cultures were impacted were dramatically different. The people on the good team are looking for new jobs, whereas the people on the great team are co-planning their next big challenge. And ultimately, the challenging project hurt the culture at the good company, yet improved and reinforced the culture at the great company.

By choosing to intentionally manage your culture, you not only step into your fuller potential but you enable the potential in others, which all drives the business to its fullest potential (and saves money). Lofty goals or the most beautiful of business strategies are powerless without the passions, talents, and capabilities of the people doing the work. A leader who steps into their full potential will unite the head part—the business—with the heart part—the culture that shapes how people bring their passion and capacities to the strategy.

CHAPTER 5

Culture Is *Your* Job

"If your actions inspire others to dream more,
do more, and become more, you are a leader."

—JOHN QUINCY ADAMS

McKinsey published an article in September 2021, in the midst of the Great Resignation, exploring what was (and likely still is) driving people to leave their jobs. In it, they shared, "If the past 18 months have taught us anything, it's that employees crave investment in the *human* aspects of work . . . They want a renewed and revised sense of purpose in their work. They want social and interpersonal connections with their colleagues and managers. They want to feel a sense of shared identity. Yes, they want pay, benefits, and perks, but more than that they want to feel valued by their organizations and managers. They want meaningful—though not necessarily in-person—*interactions*, not just transactions."[1]

If you only focus on the transactional aspects of work, people can sense it, and it's not a satisfying experience. The human aspects of work manifest most in culture, which informs how you and every person at an organization feels at the end of the day. A four-year research project led by economist Alex Edmans of the London Business School found employee well-being at certain companies preceded positive financial performance, rather than the other way around. "The 100 Best Companies to Work For in America delivered stock returns that beat their peers by 2 to 3 percent per year over a twenty-six-year period," said Edmans in a TEDx Talk on the topic. "Simply put: companies that treat their workers better do better. And this fundamentally changes the way that managers should be thinking about their workers."[2]

What conditions are you as a leader establishing that enable people to do their best thinking and then share that thinking with others? How are you creating an environment for people's actions to be meaningfully connected to the whole while also self-driven? What parameters are you setting to encourage respectful, equitable, and effective interactions between people? As a leader, you can do all that—it's your choice to create a thriving environment around you.

In fact, we argue that it's your job. If no one has said that directly to you before, we'll be very clear: culture is *your* job—it starts with you. Culture is the shadow of leadership. If you're not thinking about your role in culture, you're not taking ownership for being a true leader. Whether you're the CEO of an enterprise company or lead a small team of eight, you can choose to intentionally create a culture that fosters the thoughts, actions, and interactions that positively support your people and the business.

A LEADER'S IMPACT ON CULTURE

We have a *Fortune* 50 friend and client who has demonstrated the power of a leader stepping into his responsibility. Anthony isn't a CEO or even an SVP. He is a leader of a team that was inside a bigger team that itself was inside a bigger team. But, when he got that job, he believed he could impact and influence the people around him, and he made the choice to develop the culture on his team in an intentional way. He empowered individuals, gave them stretch opportunities, and insisted on openness and collaboration (as we know, that's not always the norm at large companies). Anthony could have said, "That's not my job" or "I'm not the CEO, what can I do?" but instead he chose a different way, a leader's way. Because he created a culture that celebrated stretch opportunities, his team believed growth was attainable in their roles, they allowed themselves to act in ways that cultivated growth (not just mastery), and their interactions with each other generated encouragement, not competition. The team worked together well and developed into leaders themselves.

Culture as the leader's choice can go another way, too. We worked with a thirty-five-year-strong financial institution that took a huge revenue and morale hit when a new CEO came on board. At around the same time the CEO started, a few leadership changes happened, too. Over a period of only a few years, the board of directors realized the culture had completely eroded. When they dug in, they realized the CEO was intentionally evoking competition among teams and instilling a set of processes and procedures that actually fractured the employees rather than bringing them together. The workplace was nothing like what it had been, yet so much of the company was still in place—only a few new people had been introduced into the mix. Luckily, the board of directors was able to take swift action to part ways with the people at the top, but then came the hard work: the slow climb back to the successful company they were before and finding a CEO whose choices would align with a foundational culture that was more empowering. And that work, that climb, was all about culture, not the business or growth strategy, and building back the trust, the clarity, and the vision that the staff could participate in and contribute to in meaningful ways.

LEADING FOR THE CULTURE YOU WANT

If you aren't cultivating a culture that is authentic and measured (so you know what's working and what's not working), you're not fully stepping into your role as a leader. You're just a manager or a boss. No offense to managers or bosses, but if you want to be a leader, too, you have to own your role in creating a workplace that actually works, that functions for both the people and the business. If the culture is lacking at a company, we've found that in most cases it's because the key leadership positions are filled with people who've never been trained or educated on what it takes to be a leader. They were good at numbers, so they rose to the role of CFO. Or they were pros at process and operations, so they rose to the position of SVP of Global Processing. But being good—or even amazing—at your domain of expertise does not mean you will be a good leader. This is a common issue at many companies. Promotions are given to people who excel at their role, not necessarily because they excel at leadership qualities.

If you believe your job is all about ten-year plans, M&A, or revenue growth but not people, this message about culture being your job might come as a rude surprise. But one drum we bang very loudly is that leaders must be shaping culture as much as they shape business plans. In "The High Cost of a Toxic Workplace Culture: How Culture Impacts the Workforce—and the Bottom Line," a 2019 study published by SHRM, they share, "Employees expect management to set the tone in the workplace, establishing its values and the communication channels necessary for managers to explain best practices and organizational goals. Approximately 3 in 4 working Americans believe management establishes workplace culture, laying the foundation for them to succeed at work."[3] People look to leaders for the signals and messages when it comes to culture around them. And when that culture isn't strong, people will simply leave in search of a better work environment. In today's competitive market there are plenty of organizations, and leaders, that do pay significant attention to developing a robust culture. Employees moving on has a cost, as the same SHRM study says, "Over the past five years, the cost of turnover due to workplace culture exceeded $223 billion." You can make all the sales you want, close all the deals you can, or have the most relevant services in your market, but if you can't manage the human energy to follow through on those products or promises, you won't achieve the level of success that you are capable of.

Of course, people need to know the *what* of your business—what you do, what the goals are, what the strategies for achieving those goals are—but they also need to know *how* they should get there. It's like the rules of engagement: What can I do and what can I not do? That's where culture comes in.

The culture you choose to establish as a leader sets expectations and boundaries about what is acceptable and unacceptable in how individuals approach their work (think), execute that work (act), and relate to one another (interact). A strong culture shows individuals how they can contribute. That allows you to get the hell out of their way and focus on empowering them to do their best work.

YOU ARE YOUR MOST POWERFUL TOOL

Now more than ever, culture has to be a top priority for the leaders of any company that wants to attract and retain talent. Jaime was in a meeting in January of 2022, and one of her peers made an observation. He asked, "Is it just us or are most of our problems right now people problems? Sales are good; people are buying. The market is strong; we feel pretty confident in our growth strategy. But people problems, they are plentiful right now."

It's so true. In the People Age, you as a leader will need to spend more time on people. And people are complex; change will take patience. The workforce environment is shifting enormously right now, and really has been for the last ten years or so. Whether you're competing against other organizations or against younger generations' interest in going out on their own, one of the primary efforts that retains people or brings new people to your company is the culture.

Our premise is that most people reading this book *aren't* hoping that their career consists entirely of clocking in, getting a paycheck, and going home. They want more, and they want their contributions to outlast their tenure. We think the same is true for many people in the workplace today. In the People Age, work can and should add meaning to people's lives. It can be a place where you get to use your strengths and ideas to contribute to the world around you, and that in turn improves your quality of life. When a work culture is strong, the workplace is more fulfilling for every employee and others around them.

While every leader defines their individual purpose differently, a spirit of wanting to make a difference or make an impact runs strong within many of the leaders we work with. And, while revenue will always be a part of business, it's rarely the detail that any individual leader will be remembered or known for.

Your role in shaping culture and your choice to make it your competitive advantage hinges on you. It's your job, but it can also be your legacy. This is the work of creating something bigger than yourself: making people feel better about coming to work, building a place in which people thrive, increasing your organization's impact in your community, and being a model for other organizations. That is all possible when you share this book or start to have even one conversation with your team.

Culture starts with you. Legacies are built from more than money; they're built from how you make people feel, how you serve your community, or how you construct a business that is resilient and lasting. These aspects of legacy are all informed by the culture you create around you.

On a personal level, if you cultivate enduring values that you continually act on and use to guide your team or the company, you create an example of a strong leader who talks the talk and walks the walk. Every person who interacts with you will take that away and potentially apply it to their own trajectory of leadership. Your legacy lives in your own thoughts, actions, and interactions—your personal culture. And you can create a ripple effect within and outside of the organization. For example, a culture with an intentional social impact focus can ripple beyond the walls of your organization and produce community benefit.

That's why you are not only on a *culture* journey; you are on a *leadership* journey. You will grow and evolve as a person as much as the culture around you if you're doing it right. Engage in the idea that you can be better—you, the team, and the organization deserve it.

EXPERT TIP:

START AT THE TOP

While culture is everyone's responsibility, starting with the leadership team and building a level of understanding and alignment with them, then expanding into an all-staff strategy works better than rolling out a new culture plan all at once. Leaders, all of them, have influence. And if there is even one skeptic who crosses their arms and digs their heels in when the CEO espouses the virtues of culture at an all-hands meeting, that person can taint the whole effort. So start with the core leadership team as you explore your Culture Climb. Take as much time as necessary to agree to the investment and the effort. Waiting for agreement might feel like it slows things down, but it's far more efficient to do it that way than to try to win more people over later after the skeptic's example has been set.

*Head to our website for tools to help you have a discussion with your leadership team: www.thecultureclimb.com.

PART II

How
High-Impact
Culture Works

As we talk about in chapter 2, culture is not any one thing; it's all the parts that go into fostering a strong and shared business strategy, cultivating present and humble leadership, and supporting all the people who interact with your business. When we expand our understanding of culture to include all the organizational and human needs, we have a much clearer picture of how culture drives results.

Our depiction of the key components of culture that leaders can affect is captured in the Impact Model, repeated here.

Having the components divided into layers that are stacked on top of each other is an intentional choice. While in theory you can work on any of these components in any order, each layer builds on the ones below it. So, for example, you will have an easier time making changes at the upper levels if you have the foundational elements in place or will have an easier time of addressing the team level if you're confident that the foundational and organizational levels are functioning well.

In the following chapters, we walk through each layer of the Impact Model, explain what the components mean, and explain how to work on that level if you think it's an area where you need to improve. (In part III, we show you tools for doing a more formal diagnosis of your culture based on the Impact Model.)

CHAPTER 6

The Anchor and Foundation of a Vibrant Culture

*"Leadership is not about title, position or flowcharts.
It is about one life influencing another."*

—JOHN MAXWELL

FIGURE 6.1. The foundational-level building blocks from the Impact Model

The foundational blocks support all the other dimensions of culture. Let's go back to our metaphor of climbing. Suppose you're going to take an overnight climbing trip. You can imagine that you need to have a few basic tools in place before you embark. This includes things like food and water, a map, a working headlamp, some ropes, and a warm sleeping bag. These all meet basic needs, and you wouldn't make it past day one without them. If somehow you did manage to climb the first day without water or sleeping, you'd taper off and lose energy on day two, and eventually, you'd have to turn around and regroup.

The foundational building blocks of the Impact Model are *that* crucial if you want to make progress toward a better future. The foundational elements encapsulate the where and what (vision), the why (purpose), and the how (values) of your company, the basics of how to share that (communication) to build a collective experience (trust), and who creates the drive, direction, and momentum (leadership).

If you don't have the foundational building blocks in place, it's a do-not-pass-go scenario. We talk more about why each of these building blocks is what we consider a foundational element, but as a quick example, consider "empowering values." If your values are not specific, if they do not reflect the organization's true nature, or if no one knows what they mean, it's difficult for employees to use them to guide their behaviors. And suppose no one is using values to guide their behaviors. In that case, everyone is simply acting however they want, not following the shared values that should set the parameters of what's acceptable and what's not at your workplace.

The same is true of your vision: if no one understands what it is or their role in helping to reach it, people's efforts will be all over the place. One person might be selling to the wrong clients, and another might be trying to build a product that has nothing to do with the ten-year plan.

Let's consider each of these components in more depth.

CONSCIOUS LEADERSHIP
IS YOUR ANCHOR

Conscious Leadership   ANCHOR

Through many sessions with teams and leaders, we've discovered that most leaders were never taught what *leadership* really is. Many leadership job descriptions don't include these qualities or expectations; they focus on the business outcomes, not the personal or interpersonal outcomes that leaders are responsible for. Leadership isn't about you, but it *starts* with you: who you are as a whole human is who you are as a leader. Helping grow and nurture whole people, yourself and others, *is* leadership.

Conscious leadership is the most foundational block because leaders impact every single aspect of culture. Yep, each one. Conscious leadership is the glue that holds everything together. What leaders do (or don't do) dictates so much about what other people do or don't do at the organization. People pay attention to their leaders; they watch them and often know what kind of mood they're in before even saying a word. People observe leaders in their organization and, on some level, take note, categorizing each behavior into buckets like "I should do that more," "never do around the boss," or "wish I could be more like that." That sphere of influence means a conscious approach to leading must be an integral part of how a leader and leadership team manage culture.

We share that culture is the leader's choice, your choice, yet your *approach* to culture is as important as choosing to focus on it in the first place. That's why conscious leadership is at the base of the model. Conscious leadership means that you have self-awareness of how your actions and behaviors impact everyone around you, including your employees, peers, managers, customers, and vendors. It's being aware that asking employees questions rather than solving their problems can empower autonomy and growth. It's knowing that if you expect respect *from* everyone, you must also show respect *for* everyone. If you, as a leader, don't hold yourself or your peers on the leadership team accountable, it is unlikely that anyone else in the company will try and hold themselves or others accountable. What leaders do, everyone else follows. A conscious leader will embody the mindsets they want to see used by teams and individuals. They will lead by example by consistently exhibiting the actions and interactions that they want to see in others. Behaving in the ways you want others to is a defining aspect of leadership.

A conscious leader can say:

- I am candid with my thoughts and ideas.

- I encourage my individual team members to be leaders regardless of their position or title.

- I actively work to recognize and understand the emotions of my team members.

- I actively listen and ask authentic questions of my team members.

- I am focused on the greater good of the team and organization.

- I regularly express my appreciation to my team members and others in the organization.

- I am committed to my own learning and development.

- I care about each team member as a human being, not just as an employee.

- I am self-aware of my own strengths and maximize the use of them.

- I have inspired my team members to discover and maximize their own strengths.

- I can recognize and name my feelings and manage them in situations.

The first part of stepping into your role as a conscious leader is becoming more aware of your behaviors—the thoughts, actions, and interactions you engage in. The self-awareness piece is key because no one is perfect, yet we just said that leaders impact every aspect of culture.

The next part of stepping into conscious leadership is recognizing the very human element of leadership. So, you're not perfect, but you're also always influencing and creating a ripple effect. That's a lot of pressure, and ultimately, no leader will always be in the mental state to handle everything exactly in a textbook way. We're human! But self-awareness will help you know how you're impacting others and help you predict your own behaviors.

Integrating conscious leadership into your culture grows the expectation and understanding that every leader has to develop and nurture people, not just produce business outputs. That's not always easy for people under pressure to hit goals, close sales, or grow revenue. We get it: humans are messy! Yet suppose you or other leaders at the top of your organization don't know your agreed-upon organizational leadership philosophy. In that case, none of your supervisors and managers will be building those skills and cultivating that culture on their respective teams or within their functional disciplines. Conscious leadership can become the core undercurrent guiding the rest of your culture. When all leaders embrace a conscious leadership philosophy and commit to self-awareness and fostering human capacity, your environment starts to shift. You start to see more of people and from people—from leadership to new hires.

How you present yourself to others and whether you are willing to examine your actions will set the tone for and shape organizational and team dynamics. Use the statements above describing what a conscious leader does to help you practice awareness. Review each one to determine if the statement is true for you. Return to each point regularly to gauge your progress. Your answers will likely evolve and change over time—we're never stagnant (nor perfect, as we mention).

CLEAR STRATEGIC VISION

Clarity of Strategic Vision	Inspiring Purpose	Empowering Values	Intentional Communication	TRUST	FOUNDATION

How well do you, as a leader, understand your company's vision? Where are you going and how will you get there? Can you easily articulate priorities and strategies for keeping your people and operations focused on those priorities? Can every person at your organization also articulate the vision and understand how they can contribute to achieving it? That may sound like a lot to rattle off. Still, when all people at an organization can describe its vision and their role, that means they know the overall direction of the organization and the unique, specific, and actionable ways to get there together.

For a quick example that most of us will recognize, let's look at Amazon's vision: to be the world's most customer-centric company. In one short sentence, employees (and others) know it's a global organization and that customers and customer-related experiences are important. The word "most" in there hints at the competitiveness and dominance that Jeff Bezos is known for.

For another example, IKEA's vision is to "create a better everyday life for the many people." And here, we have a very different understanding of where and how a company will achieve its vision. "Everyday life" tells you they focus on daily items, not rocket ships or luxury yachts. "For the many people" suggests accessibility and scale. The clarity of Amazon's and IKEA's statements can guide people sitting at their computers or standing in a warehouse as they perform their duties, have new ideas, or solve problems.

In "Demystifying the Development of an Organizational Vision," author Mark Lipton writes, "Visions and vision statements describe possibilities, attractive futures, and unreachable dreams. Unlike goals or objectives with clearly defined, measurable ends, they take a broader perspective by implying that the vision may never be fully achieved. Visions require a dose of idealism and the ability to imagine what an organization will be like when it has solved all its nagging problems."[1] A vision is really that—something way out there. It's not something the organization can achieve in three years. A visionary wants to accomplish tremendous feats; a vision shares that dream with others.

The danger of an unclear vision or a vision without a strategic component is that no one will know where the organization is going. *Are we productizing, or are we growing our consultancy services? How are we increasing revenue without adding headcount? How can I help build the next great product when I'm tasked with administrative work? How do I fit into the big picture?* While a robust and inspiring purpose fuels and motivates, a clear vision helps orient all the energy that purpose inspires.

A clear vision is a potent driver of productivity and performance. It shouldn't provide *every* detail, just the details that clear people's minds to make creative, innovative, and collaborative decisions, all the while knowing they're headed toward the right outcome. When people have that at work, they're making decisions more quickly, sharing information more effectively, and connecting dots along the way. A sync can happen when everyone's aware of the big picture and is keeping each other on course.

Leadership within great organizations is aligned on the direction of business growth. This requires occasionally stepping away from day-to-day business and putting on visionary hats to discuss trends, strengths, and weaknesses, what direction you're headed in, and outlining how the organization will get there. Yet a strong, compelling vision alone isn't enough to activate people. You also have to be clear on the strategy that you will use to work toward accomplishing your vision and the ways that people can contribute to the strategy, and hence your vision.

For example, suppose a company is coming out of hard times where layoffs and organizational reshufflings were common. Employees live in fear that no matter how well they do their jobs, they may still be unemployed next week or next month. The company decides to commit itself to a vision of being a workplace where all employees feel they can safely express their true selves and see opportunities to grow and advance. Their strategy for achieving that vision includes focusing on the organizational components of the Impact Model (accountability, systems/processes, etc.) so it stabilizes its operations, and on the anchor and foundational building blocks (especially conscious leadership, communication, and trust) to create a sense of certainty and trust with the leaders in the organization.

Being clear about where you're going, the path you're taking, and people's roles while on that path will create cultural and collective attention on your organization's North Star.

INSPIRING PURPOSE

Your purpose is *why* your organization does what it does. Purpose motivates all the employees—from the most senior to the newest person—to keep pushing forward even in the most challenging times. Purpose tethers what they do daily with deeper roots and meaning and underscores why their work matters—to them, their peers, and the external community.

Like your values, you must operationalize your purpose to make it work for your culture. It can't simply be a statement you repeat at annual meetings or only bring up in interviews when hiring for a new role and hoping to energize the prospective employee. Your purpose should validate and explain major decisions and help employees make sense of those decisions.

We had a client company that was decades old and, throughout that time, had maintained the same purpose: to provide technology solutions that propel companies. Their business wasn't about the basic day-to-day technology like phones; they focused on helping companies with upgrades and updates that advanced their clients' systems. Oh, and they had an office supply division. Did you just do a double take? We did. Why did they have an entire division devoted to something so misaligned with their purpose? The honest answer is that it was mostly a holdover from the "we can do that, too" early days. But as they grew and articulated their vision and purpose more and more, that misalignment became more prominent. They eventually divested that part of their company, which was tough. Still, once the company's purpose became clearer, leadership could explain how the decision came about to divest the office supply division and how doing so was the best outcome for the company's future. Such a radical change for everyone was made a little easier by ensuring that that change's outcomes aligned with their higher purpose.

In reality, an unclear purpose or a purpose that isn't used to drive decisions confuses people. Take the example we just described. If that company's focus was technology, how do you think the office supply employees felt each day? They didn't know how their individual contributions dovetailed to why the company existed. And the other employees in the tech divisions couldn't possibly see how the office supply wing was anything more than a drag on the overall priorities. That doesn't mean there was tension between specific individuals. It just means that there was a lot more fuzziness than clarity when it came down to the *why*—which needs to be crystal clear to motivate people.

Often, purpose gets discussed and thrown around in strategy sessions with leadership teams. In these small, higher-ups-only meetings, leadership takes action or makes decisions using the purpose, gives each other high-fives for being so purpose driven, and then walks out the door, never to bring up that process—or rationale—with the rest of the company. And here we are back to communication and conscious leadership: It is a leader's job to consistently use purpose not only to make decisions but also in how you message those decisions outward. This is how people connect with it personally, how they soak up what that purpose looks like in practice, and how you build credibility. According to McKinsey & Company, "People who live their purpose at work are more productive than people who don't. They are also healthier, more resilient, and more likely to stay at the company. Moreover, when employees feel that their purpose is aligned with the *organization's* purpose, the benefits expand to include stronger employee engagement, heightened loyalty, and a greater willingness to recommend the company to others."[2]

The credibility piece is more crucial than ever with today's workforce. Millennials and Gen Zers compose more and more of the employed workforce, and purpose is super important to them. And these days, it's not just true for the younger generations; all generations are realizing there's more to life than just getting a paycheck. If they're going to be doing something every day, there has to be a greater purpose behind it. As an organization and leader, you can start to offer that purpose in how they spend their forty-plus hours each week.

DATA DETOUR

CREATING AN INSPIRING CULTURE GETS YOU 125% MORE PRODUCTIVITY.

In *Time, Talent, Energy: Overcome Organizational Drag & Unleash Your Team's Productive Power*, published by *Harvard Business Review Press*, the authors Michael Mankins and Eric Garten state, "Our research suggests that an employee who is satisfied with his or her work is 40 percent more productive than an unsatisfied one. But an engaged employee is 44 percent more productive than a satisfied worker, and an employee who feels inspired at work is nearly 125 percent more productive than a satisfied one."[3] Purpose inspires people. Imagine getting 125% more from people? Work culture is what generates and fuels satisfaction, engagement, and inspiration. Purpose inspires people.

EMPOWERING VALUES

Values are the heart and soul of your organization. They encapsulate the DNA of who and what you are. As such, they should guide every major people decision, such as hiring, promotions, firing, and every company decision, such as who you work with, who you purchase from, and where you give time and money. Most importantly, values are the lens through which any difficult business decision should be viewed, such as how you operate, where your offices are, and what products and services you will or will not pursue. Yes, that's just about everything. When you go back to culture being the way people think, act, and interact, your company values set the core parameters for those behaviors. They are the front lines of how people understand what is possible, allowed, encouraged, and celebrated at your organization.

Values need to be real, specific, and truthful representations of what the organization cares about the most and *how* it cares. They need to have some meat to them. In "Make Your Values Mean Something," a *Harvard Business Review* article, Patrick Lencioni writes, "Most value statements are bland, toothless, or just plain dishonest. And far from being harmless, as some executives assume, they're often highly destructive. Empty value statements create cynical and dispirited employees, alienate customers, and undermine managerial credibility."[4] Values are *that* important.

DATA DETOUR

ORGANIZATIONAL VALUES GUIDED 75% OF WORKING AMERICANS DURING THE PANDEMIC.

A 2021 study by the Society for Human Resource Management (SHRM), titled "The Culture Effect: Why a Positive Workplace Culture Is the New Currency," found that 74% of working Americans claim their organizational values helped guide them through the pandemic.[5] People use values daily, sometimes consciously, and at other times subconsciously. But they use them to feel purposeful, inspire themselves, and orient themselves during tough times, like this study shows.

We have found that most organizations have relatively shallow values—not on purpose, of course, but because values are hard to create with the depth they need to have impact. Shallow values don't capture a specific or differentiating spirit; it's like they could describe any number of organizations. Take honesty as an example. It seems that to get hired and stay employed at nearly any organization, one would have to be honest. If you're caught lying, probably not good. If you're caught plagiarizing or making up data, that's likely cause for concern. Effective values that establish clear expectations have to go deeper than "honesty."

The deeper your values are, the more they will capture what your organization means and how you want those attributes to show up in actions or thoughts. You have to design them deliberately. You can't just sit in a room and list off a handful of words that sound nice (that's a fast track to empty values). You have to align the values to how you want work to be done at your organization—remember these are the DNA. You want them to be part of everything from the biggest decisions to the smallest, off-hand interactions. To show you what we mean, Table 6.A shows examples of values some of our clients had before working with us, and how we helped shape them to be more meaningful.

TABLE 6.A: SUPERFICIAL VERSUS DEEP VALUES

ORIGINAL VALUE	REFINED VALUE
Teamwork	WE before ME, or Do more together
Quality	Design it like you own it
Focused on results	We win together
Integrity	Do the right thing
Exceed expectations	Exceed the standard
Creativity	Draw outside of the lines

When they are side by side, it's easy to see the original values are generic and uninspiring; the refined versions are more specific to the company and aspirational. They differentiate the organizations by getting specific; they can more easily drive behaviors by embodying meaningful principles. Moreover, you can see how the new values can help guide employee behaviors and decisions; they won't just be posters on a wall.

OPERATIONALIZING YOUR VALUES

We've found that most leaders in most companies know how important it is to establish specific values. But operationalizing them is even more challenging than defining them. It might be easy to say that "we before me" is a core value, but when the high-performing CFO routinely goes rogue and leaves people out of key projects, that's when everyone finds out that "we before me" is lip service and not a core value because it doesn't apply equally to everyone. Does your CEO talk to the CFO about the importance of "we before me"? If not, your value is, at best, not operationalized and, at worst, a flat-out lie. If you work with the CFO and help them develop strategies for making sure their actions embody "we before me," you're living—and operationalizing— the values. That's what you're aiming for. And everyone is watching—if you don't follow through, people lose trust in the values and leadership as a whole.

To help operationalize values, we recommend defining associated behaviors that represent ways people could live into that value. For example, one of our values at Keystone is "We maximize our superpowers." We want every person who works at Keystone to be using their most significant strengths as much as possible, and we do the following to operationalize this value:

- We help every employee identify their superpower.

- We communicate our superpowers with each other.

- We hold each other and the organization accountable for using individuals' superpowers as much as possible.

- We proactively make business decisions about *who* is responsible for *what* based on their superpowers.

It's not that every single action we ever take is tied directly to our super-power. Still, we are attentive to what activities give some people energy and zap others'. We check in with each other if someone is spending too much time on tasks unrelated to their superpower because we know we're better off as a whole when we're each contributing using our highest and best use. Because we've defined desired behaviors based on this particular value, we all know we can take action accordingly.

Effective, specific, and motivating values contribute to a sense of autonomy and self-direction for all staff. Using them as guardrails for decision-making eliminates the stress and pressure of the question always nagging people at work: "Am I going to make a wrong decision?" If they use the organization's values and are in alignment with the organization's purpose, they can't make a wrong decision. Things may not turn out as expected or hoped for, but the employee can't be *wrong* if their decisions and choices align with organizational values. Making a decision in line with the company's values alleviates that fear and allows the employee to engage with the decision and outcomes in a more confident yet defined way. As a leader, if you know people are using values that are truly meaningful and accurate to your organization to guide their behaviors and decisions, you can step back and let them decide away.

EXPERT TIP:

VALUES CAN ENABLE PEER-TO-PEER COACHING

Values provide a shared language for all people in an organiza-tion. Shared values give them tools for helping each other (and themselves) when making decisions, giving feedback, or taking action. The values, when posed as questions, are a litmus test. Take "design it like you own it," for example. One employee may ask another employee, "Is this something you would put your name on? Would you go out into the world and claim this is the best *you* can do?" By using the language of the values, the two employees can engage in a discussion that feels less personal, and more about the shared mission. This fosters trust between peers and democratizes feedback—a win for leaders and staff.

INTENTIONAL COMMUNICATION

Clarity of Strategic Vision	Inspiring Purpose	Empowering Values	Intentional Communication	TRUST	FOUNDATION

Of all the problems we see grow out of inconsistent culture, poor communication is the most common. In employee feedback and roundtables, we hear about ad hoc communication or muddled (and mixed) messages that leave people with more questions than answers. Upon discussions with leadership teams, we find that many have no annual, quarterly, monthly, or weekly cadence to their messaging and don't carefully consider questions like the following: What are we trying to accomplish with our communication? How are we going about it? When are we doing it? Who is it going to, and who is sharing it? Worse yet, we find that some leaders don't even have regular communication between each other or their people. Sometimes leadership team meetings are only on an "as needed" basis (which means they are always triage meetings), or leaders simply don't take the time to go and casually talk to people about what's going on. These formal and informal practices all create a distinct feeling at an organization.

Furthermore, when you think about it, almost all communication in a business setting is about or may result in change. Say you're communicating about adding new people, pivoting in a new direction, reorganizing teams, observing market fluctuations and implications, congratulating or recognizing accomplishments. All of those messages can be interpreted as change. Every message from a leader or a leadership team raises questions in people's minds: *What does this mean? How does this impact me? What now and what's next?* This is natural and predictable and underscores the importance of intentional communication. So, whether you're aware of it or not, communication is often done in the service of change management. What you say and how you say it should assume the very human questions, and answer them, so people feel considered and clear on what's happening. That's why being intentional about communication is so important to building a positive culture.

Intentional communication helps *everyone* in an organization. It takes a little more time and planning, but the benefits are tenfold. From a productivity standpoint, intentional communication can help people know what channels to use for different types of information, how to share their own messages, and where to look when they have a question. Finding a regular cadence and demonstrating a commitment to transparency cuts down on gossip, builds trust, and allows people to believe that their questions will be answered in due time. By exhibiting intentional information sharing, you model that behavior for others. We've all seen how negative cultures can get when individuals hoard information, leading to a lack of trust, collaboration, and collective progress. If leadership behaves transparently and empathetically, information hoarders will see that behavior as necessary for success in your organization. Last, well-considered communication builds connections. Informal and formal communication is how we learn to understand each other, our environment, organization, and industry.

Communication is truly the vehicle that drives every aspect of your business—the what, why, and where are all shared in how and when you communicate. Intentional communication is the only way to build the cultural understanding and collectiveness that will achieve what you want to achieve and create the conditions and motivations for people to get you there.

SHAPING INTENTIONAL COMMUNICATIONS

Intentional communication is rooted in two primary outcomes that are great for business, though not always achieved: transparency and empathy. Intentional communication includes the tactical cadence and thoughtful clarity of how information moves within teams, between teams, and through the organization as a whole.

To develop your intentional communication skills, start by figuring out what to say. The goal should always be about transparency. Sharing as much as you can might sound like overload, but it's what employees want and need. Slack, a business communication platform, conducted a Future of Work study in 2018 that found "80% of workers want to know more about how decisions are being made by their employers." And before you think, "We got this, we're transparent!" it's important to add that "while 55% of leaders believed their organizations were very transparent, just 18% of their employees agreed."[6] To get as clear and transparent about what you're actually sharing, ask yourself or your team:

- Why are you sharing this message with the organization?

- What do you want people to believe after you share this message?

- What is the action you want people to take from this information?

But that isn't all the work. The answers to the above questions help you figure out *what* you're messaging, not *how* you will share it. Next, you want to think about what you want people to believe, understand, feel, and do with the message. This requires context and really putting yourself into people's shoes, (i.e., empathy). To build context and empathy, continue to shape the message by answering these questions:

- **What will happen?**—Include information that you know to be fact and can confidently share.

- **What's uncertain at this point or what we can't yet discuss?**— Include information that is unknown at this point. Admitting vulnerability and sharing what you don't know is crucial for empathetic communication. First, people want to understand what is unknown. Second, you establish that it's okay not to know everything yet still move forward.

- **What will NOT happen?**—Include information that you are confident will not happen, thinking about areas of rumor or fear for your employees. This will help you to stop the rumor mill with facts.

- **How can people help?**—Suggest how your team can support the organization. When people feel like they can help, they tend to be more engaged and less stressed. Moreover, helping satisfies a basic human desire to feel like we have some control of and role in what's happening.

A message that shares all of that information will be transparent and empathetic. It will share what you know and help people understand what to do, think, and feel about the message.

TRUST

As we come to the last foundational building block, consider trust the final quality to cultivate to achieve meaningful outcomes. In fact, trust is the cornerstone of *all* aspects of culture. Let's quickly review the definition of trust because that word gets thrown around a lot in culture talk, but we don't often pause to think about why it's so fundamental. To trust means to have a "firm belief in the reliability, truth, or ability of someone or something."[7]

Consider a construction company and the importance of trust on-site. If someone engages in dangerous behavior, like a leader not wearing a hard hat while walking around, employees in a trustful environment would ask them to put one on or follow the appropriate feedback chain. This ultimately reduces physical and financial risk (if something happened to that leader, the company would be on the line). Now, we're not all in physically dangerous environments, but there are opportunities that companies are missing out on wherever there is low trust. No CEO, board of directors, or staff wants that.

A lack of trust erodes performance because it creates blockers, blind spots, and liabilities. It simply causes a lot of wasted time and energy. If trust is missing from your company, you might see behaviors like territorialism, silos, an inability (or unwillingness) to collaborate, and self-limiting, which means people won't take action or make decisions out of fear of messing up or doing something wrong. Perhaps people won't speak up if they notice something odd or potentially damaging because they fear what might happen.

These are all signs trust is missing, but what does a presence of trust look like?

- Healthy conflict
- Divergent thinking
- All ideas are welcome
- Clear, proportionate, and consistent punishment for unacceptable behaviors

If you don't have a foundation of trust, you can't improve any of the other aspects of culture because every relationship within an organization is based on trust. People must believe that the organization is reliable and truthful in what it is saying and doing. Teams must believe in individuals' abilities to make decisions and do the work. Customers and clients must believe that the product or service—and the business—is what it says it is. Trust must be flowing between the organization, leaders, employees, customers, teams, and divisions. These groups need to trust each other—believe in each other—for any workplace to operate effectively.

A high level of trust improves performance and efficiency. In a high-trust company:

- Healthy conflict and disagreement are accepted and even encouraged across business units and up and down the proverbial ladder. Anyone can point out a flaw or potential issue with an idea.

- The entire organization is also encouraged to critique and to show divergent thinking. There is no way for an organization, or people, to thrive if everyone thinks alike. Plus, groupthink limits innovation. Ideas should come from all parts of the organization. Every individual has access to different information and experiences; a trustful organization (and leaders) recognizes this and encourages everyone to contribute their insights.

- The punishment for unacceptable behaviors is clear, proportionate, and consistent. Getting fired for making a typo is a disproportionate punishment. Getting put on a performance review plan for not hitting key goals for the third month in a row is proportionate. Treating a support employee the same as a top salesperson is consistent and fair. If the repercussions for unwanted behavior are clear, proportionate, and consistent, you will see more expressions of your culture because there will be less fear.

One reason high-trusting environments achieve results like that may be because as you build and develop trust, you're also building and developing psychological safety. Trust is an input, or an ingredient of, a psychologically safe environment. According to Amy Edmundson, who coined the term and has done extensive research about it, psychological safety "describes individuals' perceptions about the consequences of interpersonal risks in their work environment. It consists of taken-for-granted beliefs about how others will respond when one puts oneself on the line, such as by asking a question, seeking feedback, reporting a mistake, or proposing a new idea."[8]

The distinction between trust and psychological safety is that trust is often cultivated between two elements—person to person, person to organization, etc. Psychological safety is cultivated at a group level; it's a team dynamic that fosters individual expression and willingness to share one's perspective or opinion without fear of alienation, retribution, or judgment. But both are about candor and care, and this starts with you as the leader. While psychological safety is an entire topic on its own, it's crucial to consider that humans must feel safe to contribute to any environment fully, and trust is how you can start establishing that safety.

THE POWER OF TRUST

We're not the only ones who have this strong opinion of trust. One of the first concepts we introduce to leadership teams embarking on their Culture Climb is from Patrick Lencioni's *The Five Dysfunctions of a Team* (100% recommended reading for everyone!). The concept is Lencioni's distillation of what teams need to be functional, presented in a pyramid. Trust is the base layer, then conflict, commitment, accountability, and results are layered in that order on top of trust. You can easily compare it to Maslow's hierarchy of needs: the base layer must be met before you can get to any other layer. And "results" is the *final* layer.

The reality is that most leaders focus on results: the top of the pyramid, the finish line, the financial outcomes, the bottom line. But we want to encourage you to put all your energy into building a strong degree of trust in the organization. Doing so breeds positive conflict, improves your ability to have healthy discussions and debates about different ideas and perspectives, and develops better solutions for the organization. When individuals participate in healthy discussion and debate, their commitment to whatever comes out of that discussion increases because they were involved in the journey. The commitment then drives accountability because when a person feels committed to something—a plan, a project, an outcome—they want to follow through and for it to be successful.

All this happens when you first focus on trust at the highest level of the company, and it's practiced and cultivated at every level throughout. The outcomes speak for themselves. People's experiences at high-trust companies differ dramatically when compared to experiences at low-trust companies. They report "74% less stress, 106% more energy at work, 50% higher productivity, 13% fewer sick days, 76% more engagement, 29% more satisfaction with their lives, 40% less burnout."[9]

CREATING A SOLID FOUNDATION

As you embark on your climbing journey, the first step has to be establishing a strong foundation for all the other work that is to come. To quickly recap, you need the following:

- **Conscious leadership**, so you and the broader leadership team can model the behaviors and principles integral to your organization and culture.

- A **clear vision** gives everyone something to strive for together and propels the individuals and the organization forward.

- **An inspiring purpose** can motivate people to contribute to the forward momentum because they can see themselves in something bigger than the current moment or their singular role.

- **Empowering values** establish guardrails for behaviors and decisions so individuals can play well, yet independently, with each other.

- **Intentional communication** ensures you consider transparent messages and empathetic messaging, so people feel aware and included.

With all these foundational blocks operating well, you will create **trust** and solidify a strong belief in leadership and the organization.

EXPERT TIP:

LEADERSHIP STARTS WITH TRUST

As a conscious leader, trust is the first aspect of culture you should pay attention to and start developing personally. From a skills standpoint, it's crucial to be aware that you build trust through every thought, action, and interaction, and to understand, in every moment, how you're impacting individuals and the team. Once you start building trust, you must determine if it's working: Are people taking risks, openly sharing failures/mistakes, innovating with one another, respectfully pushing back/debating with you as the leader? If so, trust is present; if not, you must be more deliberate in efforts to develop trust.

Organizational hierarchy can get in the way of true, mutual trust, so continuously keep your antennae up for how your actions as a leader may be creating trust or distrust; trust starts with you being authentic, being real, being you. People can sense an inauthentic leader immediately. Look for trust between you and your team members, other leaders, and other teams. As a leader you should look to build trust across business units, teams, and locations. Trust with leaders (or leadership trust) is the glue that holds all the building blocks together to create a strong culture and a successful organization. It is not an option; it is a necessity.

CHAPTER 7

The Organization

"Customers will never love a company
until the employees love it first."

—SIMON SINEK

FIGURE 7.1. The organizational-level building blocks from the Impact Model

With the foundational elements in place, we can now look at the building blocks that make up the organizational layer of culture. These cultural blocks help build a strong organization and build the relationship between the organization and its stakeholders, from employees to the community.

ACCOUNTABILITY

Accountability is one of the most important building blocks of a high-performing culture. When people are accountable, they take ownership of their responsibilities. They own their actions, follow through on what they say they will do, and are able and willing to hold themselves and others accountable. Deadlines are hit, problems are solved proactively, and progress is made across different priorities because people are focused on their core tasks. When accountability is strong, people's thoughts, actions, and interactions will be in line with the organization's goals and outcomes because they will also feel ownership of the outcomes and performance of the organization as a whole. Do you remember the pyramid we describe from *The Five Dysfunctions of a Team* (p. 79)? Accountability was right below results—you can't get results if you don't have accountability. Period.

INCREASING ACCOUNTABILITY

A critical factor in building accountability is being crystal clear on people's actual accountabilities. That seems pretty obvious, right? We often see job descriptions that include many tasks, and org charts that list all the roles and titles, but accountabilities can fall through the cracks. We tell our clients to document three to five jobs that each person should obsess over. What tasks should Shana in accounting wake up wanting to achieve or improve? What are specific duties people can take responsibility for that also directly contribute to larger, organizational outcomes? What is each person absolutely, buck-stops-here responsible for? For example, on a sales team, one person might have "leads generated from the website" as an accountability. Their efforts, experiments, and energy are directed toward website lead gen. If someone else has an idea about how to increase leads, they know who to talk to. If web leads dry up, the team knows who is accountable to get the numbers back up.

An organizational accountability map, which is like a souped-up org chart, delineates who owns what so they can hold themselves accountable, their leaders can hold them accountable, and everyone can hold each other accountable. When intrinsic and extrinsic accountability come together, a true culture of accountability starts to grow. Individuals are motivated by their ability to see how their daily work contributes to the bigger objectives. They trust that there is value in and permission to hold others accountable. Everyone believes that it will help the organization as a whole when they act according to the responsibilities on the accountability chart.

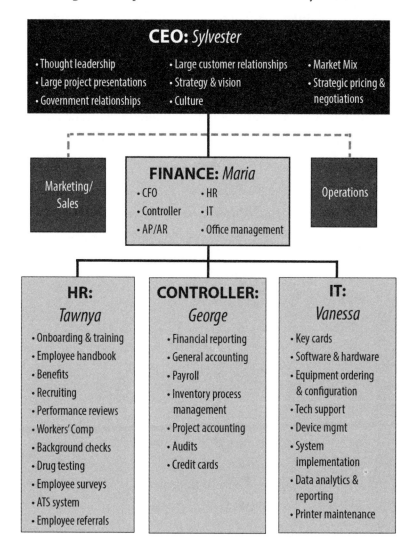

FIGURE 7.2. Organization accountability map image
This excerpt shows the multiple layers that compose an organizational accountability map. As you can see, each block lists the organizational role or division plus the accountabilities associated with that block.

After accountabilities are determined, don't tuck that organizational accountability map away into a rarely viewed intranet folder! You now have to share that information across the entire organization so everybody, and every team, is crystal clear on who does what (this is intentional communication in action). This eliminates finger-pointing—if it's on Sarah's accountability list, it doesn't matter if Dave over in finance forgot to send Sarah a document. It's on her to either follow up and ensure she gets what she needs or to hold him accountable.

The final step is to review accountabilities and ownership frequently. Treat your functional accountability chart as a living, real-time document that should provide genuine motivation for people. In his book *Drive*, Daniel Pink found that autonomy, mastery, and purpose are core to personal motivation. He summarizes these qualities as the following:

- Autonomy: the desire to direct our own lives.

- Mastery: the urge to get better and better at something that matters.

- Purpose: the yearning to do what we do in the service of something larger than ourselves.[1]

Clear, up-to-date, and well-constructed accountabilities enable each of these behaviors. Once you know what you're supposed to do, you can focus on the "how" (autonomy). Because it's your obsession and you know it directly impacts the organization, you want to do it well and see it through (mastery and purpose). Minimally, leaders should review their own and their teams' accountabilities annually and ask, "Are these still accurate for the coming year?" and "Is there an opportunity for any of my employees to grow into larger responsibilities or be promoted into a new role?" And ask the people if they feel like they are motivated by the accountabilities.

Once you operationalize accountabilities—clear, shared, and practiced—workflow and working together become so much easier. No one has to wonder, "Should I bring up how Dave has missed a few deadlines?" The answer to that question will be clear: yes. They will walk over and ask, "Hey Dave, I've noticed a few deadlines have come and gone. Are you doing okay?

How can we help you keep attention on your highest-priority tasks?" It's not personal, and it's not about blame. A culture of accountability is about clear communication and mutual responsibility—it's on *all of us* to ensure we're participating. It's easy to see why high performance is achieved when a strong sense of accountability runs through a work culture. People are getting things done because they are clear about what to focus on, and if there is an issue, people know who to talk to, and they trust they will be heard.

EXPERT TIP:

UNDERSTAND THE RELATIONSHIP BETWEEN TRUST AND ACCOUNTABILITY

Trust and accountability have a symbiotic relationship. Trust is necessary for accountability—people have to trust that others will be accountable for their own responsibilities and trust that they can point out if someone isn't. In low-trust cultures, accountability will likely also be low. And yet, focusing on building a strong culture of accountability can also build trust. As you gain clarity around who is accountable for what, it empowers people to own their actions, and as more people do this, individuals will start to trust each other more and trust themselves to accomplish what they need to.

SYSTEMS + PROCESSES

Business systems are the inner workings of your operations and are made up of subsystems and processes that allow your organization to run efficiently. When the systems are effective, they help you consistently achieve your business goals. We know systems and processes may sound boring (except to you ops people—shout out to all you who love to dig into this!); it's like the plumbing or electrical systems in your home—not the interesting stuff. Yet systems and processes are the lifelines of your business. They keep everything and everyone wrangled, as they impact a ton of people and interactions.

Despite the importance of systems, we didn't include this building block in the first draft of our culture model. Like most organizations, we tucked systems and processes into the operational side of the business, not the culture side. But as we worked through culture assessments and culture development plans with clients, we realized how much systems and processes impact not only how people work but also how people *feel about* work. When they're clear and effective, there is an order to things. Generally, things run smoothly and the processes ease friction. And when systems are unclear, chaos results. A weak set of systems and processes leads to confusion, mistakes, disgruntled employees or frustrated managers, customer complaints, and failed communication between employees.

Systems are the big frameworks that businesses use to operate. Common systems are payroll and billing, HR management, communications, etc. These are all complex systems with many users, and they meet many needs—and often must work in sync to conduct business efficiently. A city may have a snowplow system to help them organize its efforts during snow emergencies. A hotel has a reservation system, which has both a customer-facing side and an employee-facing side. There are often subsystems and processes within every system that help the various users navigate the bigger framework: a time-logging process within an accounting system, an application process within an HR system, or a crisis communication protocol within a communication process. When the systems and processes come together, they create the tactical infrastructure that supports how things get done within an organization. That is where the chaos or the clarity comes in—a lack of systems and processes means everyone is doing something different. In contrast, clarity means people do similar things and follow similar rules.

IMPROVE SYSTEMS = IMPROVE CULTURE

Well-working systems and processes can also make work easier and more positive, whereas ineffective or burdensome processes mean people may not be getting what they need at work. One of our health care staffing clients was experiencing the pain of an ineffective performance review process that was creating more issues than it was solving. They could tell that employees were not excited about or looking forward to their annual reviews, which seldom included impactful conversations between employees and their supervisor. Meanwhile, supervisors copied and pasted content from previous years' reviews, feeling the pressure and anxiety of writing evaluations and meeting with employees. Last, the organization wasn't seeing any value from the standard evaluations; the forms had been developed years before and were never updated.

In short, the whole process had become a drag. But when done right, performance discussions can and should be highly engaged exchanges with productive outcomes for all parties. So, clearly this health care company's system was not a well-functioning process, people were suffering (and wasting time), and the business was getting little to no value from it.

We did a complete, start-to-finish system and process review. We conducted focus groups with employees and supervisors, asking what they liked, didn't like, and wished for. Using the feedback, we redesigned the whole performance process, with changes including the following:

- For cadence and impact, we ditched the high-pressure, low-relevance annual review and switched to monthly check-ins and biannual review of goals and performance.

- From a content perspective, we developed a more conversational format to encourage dialogue between supervisors and employees and added specific sections for coaching, goal setting, and celebrating accomplishments.

The new structure provided (forced, in some cases) deeper conversations, more meaningful goals aligned with the organization's strategy, and positive moments. By changing the cadence and content, the process went from an annual annoyance to a more effective employee experience—thus a more effective organizational tool. The new process, and the better interactions people had because of that new process, facilitated a stronger culture: colleagues were having more positive exchanges; by investing in a redesign, the organization demonstrated that it cared about people and their experience; and employees gained clarity on ways they could contribute.

BEST PRACTICES FOR SYSTEM DEVELOPMENT

This performance review story is just one example, and of course no two processes are alike, but there are best practices that help. For the most part, systems and processes require a few features to be effective:

- Each phase—creating, implementing, training, and iterating—of each system or process needs to have a clear owner.

- Every system or process needs a **why** that explains its purpose so users are clear on the reason for it and can understand that specific piece within the larger business context. Sure, logging time using an app might be a little annoying to a delivery team, but if they know it helps the company ensure profitability and sustainability, then they know they're contributing to an important pool of information that impacts them and all their peers.

- People have to know about and be **trained** on the process yet still have the **flexibility** to bypass steps if necessary. Yes, you read that correctly: people need to sidestep or leapfrog the process at times. Most of the time, systems and processes are great, but they don't account for every possible scenario. When outlier scenarios happen, people need to know they can do whatever they believe is best based on the organization's purpose and values, which may mean bucking the system or protocols.

When you have a balance of structure and freedom, people know the guardrails, know what is expected, and feel trusted to act in the way they see fit. As a leader, you want that give and take, that 80/20 dynamic: 80% of the time, the process is followed, and 20% of the time, people are using the "why" behind it all to make slight adaptations based on their creativity, individual capabilities, and the demands of the situation at hand. That means they are thinking, "I know what's expected of me, and I also know I have the autonomy to take different steps based on the bigger purpose." That is a great combination of feelings for people to bring to work: a sense of shared understanding and confidence that they can perform uniquely within.

SOCIAL IMPACT

I think we all know that people don't just want to sell widgets anymore. They want to participate in something bigger—and social impact is one way you offer that to them and attract them to your company. Employees and prospective employees care about how a company interacts with and builds up its community. Millennials believe companies should be actively involved in social issues, and two-thirds visit corporate websites at least somewhat often to learn about their efforts.[2] And 90% of Gen Zers believe companies must act to help social and environmental issues; 75% will research to see if a company is being honest when it takes a stand on issues.[3]

And businesses *can* achieve both profit and impact at the same time. While not the only book to have done so, *Conscious Capitalism*[4] helped popularize the idea that doing good in the world and doing good in business are not mutually exclusive. Thinking more broadly about business and moving from a shareholder mindset to a stakeholder mindset was an important shift that conscious capitalism created and is now becoming the norm. Stakeholders are everyone and everything impacted by your business: employees, employees' families, the environment, neighbors, vendors, and the individuals who make the pens you purchase. Your business can positively or negatively influence any of these stakeholders. You probably can't do right by everyone all the time, but you can develop an intentional plan to do the most good you can. When work and operations are done with a greater purpose, you attract and engage employees, boosting organizational profits and productivity. As we said, profits and impact are interconnected.

THE SOCIAL CONTRACT

All organizations have a social contract with their surrounding communities. They directly benefit from the shared community infrastructure and resources, like the streets, medical systems, or parks. And the reverse is also true. Your organization directly (though not always intentionally) impacts the community with its physical and virtual presences, like its building grounds, its social media brand and content, and how its employees engage with peers and neighboring organizations. When the company's employees exit at the end of their day, they push the door open, step out onto the sidewalk, and are members of their community. This adds another potential layer of good: the organization's leaders have the opportunity to create engaged, healthy citizens or not. Of course, the organization doesn't own all of that but influences these spheres immensely.

This social contract means all of us are impacted by and impact our social surroundings every day. Getting more intentional about your corporate social responsibility to give back and to do business in an ethical, sustainable, inclusive, and health-promoting way for people, community, and society is key to being a good corporate citizen in the twenty-first century.

Doing social good is not only good for your community, but it can also help foster a great workforce. What an organization—and its leaders— do to positively impact the world influences how its employees feel about work and their level of engagement. For example, if an organization is in the news over and over again for its failure to keep their manufacturing sites clean, thus creating toxicity in the drain water for the nearby homes, employees may start to feel negative and question the organization's value. On the other side of town, you might have a CEO who is also in the news all the time, but for her position on mentoring high school students to prepare them for more industry opportunities before college. The employees at her organization may feel energized and inspired by her and, by association, inspired by the organization, too.

Of course, the reasons for being more socially responsible and increasing your organization's positive impact aren't only about employee sentiment, retention, and brand perception. Social responsibility also creates stronger communities. Organizations have many opportunities to add goodness and positivity to the world. It could be one-off events like a coat or food drive, building a relationship with a local organization, or mentoring people who may not yet qualify for a job. Is your finance department purchasing from green companies that use sustainable practices? Are you ethical in how you broadcast and interview for your open positions? You don't have to go big when it comes to social impact. Even small efforts create a ripple of awareness and impact. And as the ripple makes its way outward, you build a company image and brand as one that cares, which helps people see your company and culture positively.

Businesses are an incredibly influential part of the social and civic ecosystem. They can leverage their positions and power to help make substantial contributions. If you want a business that flourishes and exists inside a healthy community, you should cocreate that with your employees and community. All in all, when your employees are holistically healthier, your business is healthier. When your community is healthy and thriving, your business is more likely to be healthy and thrive.

INCLUSION + BELONGING

ORGANIZATION

You've surely felt the increased focus on diversity, equity, and inclusion over the last decade, and those are all a part of ensuring people feel like they belong. Let's start here with some definitions to make sure we have a shared language.

- Diversity is having different genders, races, ages, ethnicities, abilities, experiences, knowledges, and styles present.

- Equity is not equality (giving people the same thing) but finding out and serving the different needs of each individual.

- Inclusion allows every employee to be themselves, participate fully, and contribute to the organization's success.

- Belonging is our human need to interact and connect with others and create a shared sense of identity through that relationship. A sense of belonging includes how people within a team, department, and throughout the organization relate.

We will focus primarily on belonging because it is the outcome of the other three—diversity, equity, and inclusion (DEI)—and it's what to aim for when building your DEI practice at your organization. When people feel like they belong, as they fully and wholly do, they begin to feel psychologically safe and contribute to the shared purpose that the group is working toward. Here, purpose and vision can serve a huge role in uniting all the unique and different people who desire, on a universal human level, to work together to create something. When people feel truly welcomed and accepted in their work community, they can release any limitations or fears they may otherwise bring to a conversation, interaction, or project.

They will be more likely to express their true, authentic self, which all leaders want from their people.

By developing a sense of belonging and safety, organizations allow individuals to move out of fight-or-flight mode and access the higher-functioning parts of their brain to bring their best thinking and ideas forward. We can all recall a situation where we felt like we didn't "fit in" (aka belong) with a group of people. And if we transport ourselves back to that experience, we can probably remember how much time we spent wondering what we should say, worried that our sense of humor might not come off well, or receding into the background hoping no one would speak to us. We don't want people to show up to work worrying, constantly assessing and taking stock, or silencing themselves. That limits them, and it limits the organization's potential, too.

A sense of belonging draws people to the work and allows them to share openly with the group. If individuals feel like they belong, they also trust that they can raise issues, ask questions, and contribute opinions, which all lead to higher performance as a group. As Google learned, psychological safety was a critical determinant in whether their teams succeeded or failed.[5] Having a bunch of high performers on the same team wasn't as important as having a collection of teammates who felt safe with each other.

In a recent BetterUp study, the authors found that, "High belonging was linked to a whopping 56% increase in job performance, a 50% drop in turnover risk, and a 75% reduction in sick days. For a 10,000-person company, this would result in annual savings of more than $52M."[6] And for a 100-person company, based on that calculation, the annual savings could be more than $520,000. A culture of belonging makes people *want* to contribute, work hard, and stick around. When people feel like they belong, they feel a commitment to the organization. A culture of belonging encourages openness and authenticity, which is important to work contribution. A study by Michael Slepian and Drew Jacoby-Senghor from Columbia University revealed that "when employees felt like they didn't belong in the workplace, they felt like they couldn't be themselves at work.

When employees feel they can't be their authentic self at work, they have lower workplace satisfaction, find less meaning in their work, and have one foot out the door."[7]

Creating a workplace of belonging, inclusion, equity, and diversity starts with the leader. If a leader, like yourself, is empathetic, vulnerable, and open, everyone else will feel more able to act in similar ways. People can come into work situations and be who they are. They won't mimic someone else (likely the leader). They will come in dressing however they want to dress, talking how they want to talk, approaching problems and projects how they want to. They will use their background, experiences, and individual cultures and feel comfortable talking about it, sharing it, and living it. And that contributes directly to an empowered and empowering workforce.

DATA DETOUR

A NEGATIVE CULTURE IS 10X MORE IMPORTANT THAN COMPENSATION IN PREDICTING TURNOVER.

A study published in the *MIT Sloan Management Review* found that toxic work culture was 10x more important than compensation at predicting turnover, even when adjusting for industry attrition. What makes a culture toxic? The leading contributors to toxicity include "failure to promote diversity, equity, and inclusion; workers feeling disrespected; and unethical behavior. And employees are 2.9x more likely to leave companies that fail to distinguish between high performers and laggards when it comes to recognition and rewards."[8] Not only do positive cultures attract individuals, but toxic ones also repel them.

REWARDS + BENEFITS

While rewards and benefits may not be the sexiest aspect of culture, they are crucial factors in meeting employees' basic needs. The security of paying rent or the mortgage, buying food, going to the doctor, and saving for the future all contribute to an individual's well-being. If they're worrying about basics while trying to build a spreadsheet they were asked to make, they will be distracted and unable to perform at their highest capacity.

A huge mindset shift happens when you start engaging with rewards and benefits as an aspect of your culture. Rather than viewing them as an expense, you start to understand them as investments in your people. People are your greatest asset, and how you reward them and the benefits package you offer are some ways you can express that. These are all investments in the health, well-being, recognition, and appreciation of your greatest assets. When you have a robust and thoughtful rewards and benefits philosophy and follow-through, people will feel secure, know their path or potential within the organization, and believe there are opportunities for their needs and what they value to be met.

STRUCTURED BENEFITS

Compensation, health insurance, 401(k) matching, and more represent the **structured benefits**. Structured rewards may include profit-sharing programs, annual bonuses or stock options, commissions, etc. In our experience, structured rewards and benefits are often standardized across the organization and are commonly practiced, even in organizations that have average work cultures.

What we've discovered is that *how* structured benefits are handled has a bigger impact on culture than *if* they are present at all. When we talk about rewards with our clients, we usually begin with the importance of consistency. For example, having a compensation and rewards philosophy that you regularly review and share with employees is one way to be transparent and develop trust in fairness. A philosophy outlines how your compensation sits in the market. Are you above market to attract the best of the best? Or are some roles at the lower end of the market to offer entry-level job seekers an inroad to building their careers? Some companies may offer a little less base pay but have a higher bonus potential. Some offer workday flexibility to offset a below-market base pay. What is most important is having a well-thought-out philosophy grounded in what the organization can afford and the needs and wants of the people you want to hire and who already work for you. You should know if offering pet insurance is important to your staff or if a matching-gifts program is valued and utilized by individuals. Having a package, or options, that reflect people's needs and values shows them that the organization sees them and is aligned with who they are. If you don't have a strategy or a philosophy around this, you may not meet people's basic human needs of feeling secure. And if you're not meeting your employees' basic human needs, how will you ever build a culture?

To impact your culture positively, you also have to be transparent about your approach to compensation. This one can be difficult for some leadership teams. But if you think people at your organization aren't talking about their pay, you are wrong. They do talk. If they discover discrepancies or unfairness that are either real or perceived, your morale will suffer. Suppose a new twenty-something hire makes the same paycheck as a senior staffer. In that case, the higher-seniority person may come to believe that you don't highly value their institutional knowledge and experience. Money isn't everything, but those financial transactions are one way you can express how much you value and understand the people around you.

UNSTRUCTURED BENEFITS

Now, let's focus on some less-structured benefits and rewards that play into whether people feel recognized, supported, and valued. There are fringe benefits, like snacks, drink options, bike racks, and gym equipment. Together, these can shape the character of a workplace and encourage people to come as they are. *You like to bike? Great, bike here and then grab a shower to feel refreshed. We got you!*

While fringe perks like food and amenities play a role in culture, we want to focus on appreciation, which is an unstructured part of rewards vital to culture. Creating a culture where appreciation, recognition, and gratitude are practiced taps into a very human need to feel valued. Day-to-day or project-level expressions of appreciation are important—a shout-out here, a feature blog post there, or a team day off are not always planned, but they can demonstrate a lot. These unstructured rewards often get lost in discussions about compensation and benefits. Yet, a McKinsey & Company study from 2021 found that the top three factors employees cited as reasons for quitting were the following:

- They didn't feel valued by their organizations (54%).
- They didn't feel valued by their managers (52%).
- They didn't feel a sense of belonging at work (51%).[9]

As a leader, you want to strike a balance. You want enough standardization or appreciation programs to enable the behavior you want—appreciation and gratitude! But the go-to standards can't be so rigid that people stop caring about them. Trust people and teams to show recognition in the way they believe they should show it—this allows for personalization and tailoring to that circumstance (and builds trust!). If you, or others in the organization, show gratitude and it's done in a way that aligns with what an individual or team values, you build strong connections and people feel cared for. Alternatively, if you give everyone a $25 gift card to TGI Friday's regardless of what you're celebrating or the effort, that gift of appreciation will become meaningless. Align the reward to the level of effort, the type of effort, and the people involved. This personalization is where your emotional intelligence and authentically knowing each of your people can really pay off.

GETTING THE FUNCTIONAL PIECES IN PLACE

If an organization does not function correctly, there will be no organization, let alone culture. Thousands or even millions of moving parts create a functional organization. The components we've identified at this level—accountability, systems + processes, social impact, inclusion + belonging, and rewards + benefits—represent the key areas that have the most impact on your ability to get work done. And these arenas affect culture and therefore results. You need to make sure that all these pieces fit together in ways that ensure your business can fulfill its vision, that they create a workplace where people come to work every day knowing what they are supposed to do and how to do it, and that they ensure the organization's impact both internally and externally is deliberately shaped to achieve positive outcomes.

CHAPTER 8

The Team

"A culture is strong when people work with each other, for each other. A culture is weak when people work against each other, for themselves."

—SIMON SINEK

FIGURE 8.1. The team-level building blocks from the Impact Model

Team culture can be as crucial to an employee's experience as an organizational culture overall. We often spend the most time with our teams and are influenced most by the thoughts, actions, and interactions at the team level. We've found that team cultures always have more variety than an organization because expressions of the organizational culture show up differently based on who makes up the team. Yet, consistency and structure have to be in place—and thriving—at a team level for the organization to succeed. So how do we build a culture at a team level?

PEOPLE DEVELOPMENT

People development is the set of systems and processes that include recruiting, onboarding, on-the-job training, performance reviews, and development opportunities to help people and the team enhance how they perform at their current responsibilities. It includes focusing on individual strengths while embedding the organization's purpose and core values into the team. People development is all about helping people succeed in the job they have now. It's matching people with good roles, teaching them how to do their job within the context of the larger organization, and developing new skills to improve their performance after they've nailed the table stakes.

People development must be happening at all levels of the organization. We often see leadership teams that believe development is no longer necessary because they've made it to the leadership level. We've heard teams say: *We don't need it. We've been leaders for twenty or thirty years. We can't possibly need to focus on development, collaborating, or fun . . . we're too busy running the business.* In reality, leaders need to be doing more of it as they advance and have greater responsibility. If this is how you, or people on your team, view your performance, we'd like to issue you a wake-up call: You need to grow, seek out new skills, and maybe leadership skills in particular!

In *Mindset: The New Psychology of Success*, author Carol Dweck shares her observations that mindsets can hugely impact behaviors and outcomes. She articulated two mindsets in particular: fixed and growth mindsets. "People with a *fixed mindset*—those who believe that abilities are fixed—are less likely to flourish than those with a *growth mindset*—those who believe that abilities can be developed."[1] Embracing a growth mindset means believing that you can grow, as Dweck states, but also continuously seeking to grow—your awareness, perspective, and knowledge—because there are no limits. If growth is always possible, then we're never done growing. Leaders who embody this mindset and infuse it into their leadership can set a rich stage for others to value learning and development.

HAVING A PEOPLE DEVELOPMENT STRATEGY

An effective people development strategy aligns an individual's role with their individual strengths. Every job requires core skills, but each person will also bring something that is all their own to their job. Whether you call it their superpower (like we do here at Keystone) or their unique talent, a strong culture will draw it out and encourage people to integrate their personal strengths with the set of core skills. This is where growth leads to flourishing, not just incremental improvement.

In today's competitive market, a well-defined people development strategy can be a powerful lever to attract and retain the best people. At the outset, it can be a critical selling point in your hiring process. Have you seen job posts about needing someone who can "hit the ground running" or "is very self-motivated to learn new skills"? Those can be red flags that the organization doesn't have a well-articulated talent development system. An articulated development strategy shows people how they are onboarded and trained. Instead of hitting the ground running, they'll have a runway. That's a much more appealing scenario for most high-performing people.

If you aren't defining a growth path or strategy for your employees, you'll get many people who may be developing skills and knowledge in areas that are not useful for their jobs or your organization. You need growth plans because people can't achieve a goal that isn't defined. The plans will show people how they can grow without leaving the organization. Think of your people development like a marathon training program. You don't just wake up one day and run a marathon (or learn a random new skill). To be successful, you have to train and build up your capabilities, and the training programs have to allow for individualization. One person might be a little stronger in one aspect of training and another person stronger in a different way. For example, one person might be a little stronger at speed training, so they need to work on endurance training, while another person has run multiple half marathons, so they don't need to take as long to level up their weekly mileage. Each can run a marathon using the same program and yet do it in their way with their unique abilities and quirks. People development can work the same way when done well: you give enough structure for employees to grow in ways that help them in their roles but allow each person to do it in ways that make sense for them.

When it comes to attracting and retaining strong contributors, a strong people development program will signal that you encourage their growth and expect them to continue learning throughout their time at your organization. Most people want this—few want to come in and do the same task for twenty years. Showing new recruits that you value their experience from the first day will help them stay committed to the organization as they grow. And continuous improvement among people will grow a team's capabilities, which ultimately feeds into higher performance for the organization. Last, investing in people development shows you are as committed to individuals as you want them to be committed to the organization. It shows them you care.

EXPERT TIP:

USE PERFORMANCE REVIEWS TO ENHANCE CULTURE

Performance reviews are an incredibly potent aspect of your people development because so many dimensions of your culture are at play. (We shared a story about a company's improvement of its performance review system on p. 89.) A performance review can serve as a culture contribution review in many ways. How is the person expressing the organization's values? Are they holding themselves accountable? In an intentional culture, leaders will continually be assessing people not only based on how they are executing their job but also on how they are growing and developing the cultural dimensions around them, such as purpose, communication, and vision.

INNOVATION

Few organizations want innovation for its own sake—they want the innovation ideas or solutions to be in service to the continuous growth of people and outcomes leaders are aiming for. Every organization in every industry has pain points, and innovation is the path to relieving the pain. If you ignore issues or hope someone else solves them, you both miss an opportunity and fall behind. In the case of innovation, business needs and human impulses intersect; the saying "When you stop growing, you start dying" is as true for businesses as it is for individuals.

Let's get one thing out of the way: not all innovation looks like Elon Musk or sending rockets to Mars. Innovation can happen in incremental ways in every organization, no matter how future forward or traditional. As you think about Culture Climb and getting to that next, better version of your organization, innovation will almost always be a part of the path. High-performing organizations and teams must always assess how they can adapt and change to be more effective. We have included it as a building block to remind you that innovation is more than an on-demand action or one-time event that you do at off-sites, but is instead a mindset that people carry with them, an embedded aspect of how people think and behave.

We are talking about everyday innovation—a mindset of innovation that starts with simple questions, like the following: "How can I make this better? How do we get a little bit better at this procedure? Why do these processes seem clunky, and what can we fix? How can I make this more client friendly? How can I make it less administrative? How can I automate this to make it faster?" These kinds of considerations add an ever-present character of innovation to teams.

FOSTERING INNOVATION

To foster a culture of innovation, you must reward people when they exhibit qualities such as curiosity and experimentation. Leaders must lean on the growth mindset we discuss above so instead of seeing problems and issues, your people see opportunities. The environment must uphold failure not as a bad thing, but as a learning moment: What worked? What didn't work? What can we use to build the next version of the experiment? Your people have to be encouraged to ask questions and propose new ideas versus being shot down or told there isn't time to experiment. Employees have to be recognized for trying something new, even if it doesn't work, because their intention—improvement—was worthwhile and will eventually lead to better outcomes.

Create expectations and an environment of continuous improvement by incorporating new ideas into the structure of the business: ask for thoughts, improvements, etc. at weekly team meetings, 1:1s, quarterly conversations, and annual reviews. Anytime you're trying to solve an issue, ask, "How can we step outside the box and think about this differently?" Your environment needs to be high in trust, intentional with communication, and openly collaborative in order to truly pull out innovative ideas. When you move innovation from the annual brainstorms into the behavioral practices of how people think of every aspect of their work, you will see shifts in how people feel about work. It's motivating to approach daily work with inquiries and possibility. Instead of "Why is this process like this?" they will think, "How could I make this more efficient for the team and me?" That's when the organization will reap the benefits of new ideas, and people will reap the benefits of feeling like victors, not victims, of their jobs.

FUN!

Finally, right? We're to the *fun* part, where most people's brains jump when we introduce the topic of culture. So, yes, fun is a dimension, and it's an important one. Having fun with each other at work can be extremely beneficial to performance. Of course, some fun additions at the workplace like field trips or socializing during group lunches build relationships, but many leaders forget (or maybe never learned) the impact of fun on productivity.

In the study "Happiness and Productivity: Understanding the Happy-Productive Worker," scientists had individuals participate in "fun" activities, like watching a short comedy sketch or eating snacks. Afterward, they made sure the individuals indeed enjoyed those activities (most did) and then engaged the participants in tasks. The people who had fun before their tasks were 12% more productive than the control group.[2]

Similarly, Shawn Achor, author of *The Happiness Advantage: The Seven Principles of Positive Psychology That Fuel Success and Performance at Work*, wrote, "Focusing on the good isn't just about overcoming our inner grump to see the glass half full. It's about opening our minds to the ideas and opportunities that will help us be more productive, effective, and successful at work and in life."[3] And while fun doesn't always equate with positivity, it's far more likely to result in positive feelings than, say, sitting at a desk and anxiously trying to solve complex problems all day because the pressure is so high.

When we are having fun, we do better work. We learn better and at a deeper level. We all know this based on our personal experiences. We get ideas when we go for walks or when we are relaxed and allow our brains to wander a bit. We collaborate better with colleagues we can be natural with and relaxed around. We want to work longer and harder on a project that feels like a fun challenge, not a total grind. A fun environment enables creativity, a core factor in problem-solving, which means we're often not even working harder, just differently, when we're bringing levity and fun to our daily tasks. The truth is, we're all thirsty for a relief from the pressures we have in our lives. Work can be that—not every minute of every day, but we can offer that to each other on our teams and between teams.

We can (and should) have fun in short bursts at work. Aside from enjoying work more if it's fun, it is also a way to connect with others. It can be joyful conversations before a meeting starts, a high-five you share with your teammate as you walk between rooms, or a group laugh at the picture of a coworker's three-year-old in her silly Halloween costume. In fact, that is where positivity and fun start, because if no one is having fun in occasional chats with their colleagues, they sure as heck aren't going to go to a happy hour or picnic to spend more time with those colleagues.

Leaders have a significant impact on whether fun is happening throughout an organization. If a leader is a never-leaves-the-office, nose-to-the-grindstone type, guess how much fun people think they can have? Not a lot. But if a leader says hi, lets off some steam with some friendly and fun banter, and weaves a sense of positivity throughout the day, it permits people to do the same. Bottom line: don't be afraid to have a good time! When we laugh together or engage in a goofy moment, we start to build camaraderie and care.

COLLABORATION

High levels of collaboration indicate good team chemistry and healthy levels of psychological safety. In contrast, low levels tell you that you have some deeper, maybe even foundational culture issues such as low trust.

Collaboration is such a bellwether of your culture because it requires so many other cultural dimensions to be in place for people to do it effectively. To truly collaborate, individuals need to feel:

- a sense of belonging and security that they can be their authentic selves;

- that they will be listened to and their ideas will be considered;

- that a diverse representation of roles and backgrounds is present so the group isn't engaging in groupthink;

- a belief that everyone will be accountable to the organization's values and purpose;

- a positive, fun environment that is open to and draws out new perspectives; and

- honest communication that fosters participation and inclusion.

Every organization wants a collaborative spirit in their teams because when there's collaboration, problems get solved better. "Better" might mean faster, more effectively, or more comprehensively. When there is more collaboration, we can solve more complex problems, build on each other's ideas to innovate, and communicate more freely and informally. When people truly collaborate, they use a diverse set of information, skills, and perspectives to achieve different outcomes. It also helps people learn in less formal and more hands-on ways that spark growth.

Many companies are striving for a collaborative environment given all the positives that come out of it, yet there are common obstacles. Siloing, the opposite of collaboration, can be hard to resist—for individuals, teams, and departments. Sharing information or bringing new people into the mix isn't always the easier path. It requires more communication and intentionality, but collaboration serves the human social instinct to work with others and feeds our desire to offer help when we can.

COLLABORATION REQUIRES SKILL

In the article "Cracking the Code of Sustained Collaboration," behavioral scientist Francesca Gino shares some knowledge from her research that may help reframe how you think about the topic. After interviewing dozens of leaders, she found they resoundingly value collaboration but also resoundingly have not figured out how to successfully do it. She observes, "One problem is that leaders think about collaboration too narrowly: as a value to cultivate but not a skill to teach."[4]

In other words, just because people (or you) *want* collaboration to happen doesn't mean it *will*. You have to set the conditions for it to be successful. She continues, "When I analyzed sustained collaborations in a wide range of industries, I found that they were marked by common mental attitudes: widespread respect for colleagues' contributions, openness to experimenting with others' ideas, and sensitivity to how one's actions may affect both colleagues' work and the mission's outcome." Those attitudes sound a lot like what an impactful culture can create. If you and your team embody a growth mindset and focus on building the capabilities of successful collaboration, you'll be much more successful than if you assume people will know how to do it. Take the time to cultivate both the value *and* the skills.

As an example, we had a client who found success using Kaizen-type (improvement through incremental change) activities to rethink the customer support department, teams, and processes. They invited employees and leaders from customer support, of course, but also people from sales, implementation, finance, and administration. Bringing people together from all parts of the organization allowed employees to practice collaborative skills, getting to know one another at a deeper level and understanding the diverse perspectives and experiences. By engaging in this team-based activity with a cross section of people, they not only created something impactful, but they also developed their learning and empathy skills. From an organizational perspective they saw much faster adaptation to the significant changes than they had seen in past change initiatives. Moreover, through the actions and interactions they experienced, people built new alliances and new networks of knowledge across the organization.

WORKING TOGETHER FOR FUN AND RESULTS

The team level of the Impact Model focuses on how people work *together* to achieve high performance. You need to make sure you bring the right people on board and provide them with the resources they need to thrive on the job; that you foster collaboration in pursuit of innovation; that people enjoy the workplace (more often than not!) in ways large and small. When these components come together, you will have a creative, energized workforce of people who are engaged in accomplishing common goals.

CHAPTER 9

The Individual

"You cannot teach a man anything.
You can only help him discover it within himself."

—GALILEO GALILEI

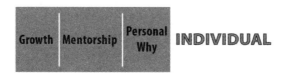

FIGURE 9.1. The individual-level building blocks from the Impact Model

As we've explored up through now, much of culture is about relationships, connections, and fostering a "we" among "I's." And yet, you can't forget the individual people and their specific needs and motivations as you create pathways from the building blocks. At the end of the day, individual contributors are doing the work. How they see themselves within the broader concentric spheres of their team, department, and organization can give them the motivation to contribute fully or can hold them back. These building blocks are how you can help people find their personal power to benefit them and the organization.

GROWTH

Previously, we discussed *people* development as helping your employees succeed in their current roles. Growth is the *personal* development building block that complements the people development building block. At the individual level, growth is all about creating an environment for people to grow as whole humans and as leaders who will support and encourage others, whatever that looks like *for that person*. It's not just about the job, the role, the skills; it's about stepping back and seeing employees as whole people who have many interests, ideas, and aspirations.

More than ever, we need to be considering each other as whole people. In a 2017 *Harvard Business Review* article, Paul Zak, author of *Trust Factor: The Science of Creating High-Performance Companies*, wrote, "High-trust workplaces help people develop personally as well as professionally." Skill building isn't enough; people also need to grow as human beings to keep performing well. Zak added, "High-trust companies adopt a growth mindset when developing talent."[1]

When you see the person's whole picture, recognize that work is just one piece of their life, and help strengthen those other areas; that recognition and strength you offer will influence their performance at work, too. When you are at work, you're still a parent, a spouse, a friend, and whatever other roles you play in your personal life. And whether you like it or not, you bring all those facets into the workplace every day. So does everyone else in your workplace. Given that reality, you might as well embrace it and make it work for you, not against you. People expect this in the workplace today; we are no longer willing to check our personal interests at the door. That's not how life works. Work/life *balance* doesn't exist anymore. Work/life *integration* is the only way to move forward. And when we do that, we allow people—as they fully are—to be authentic and to feel like they belong in our multidimensional workplaces in all *their* dimensions.

ALLOWING WHOLE-PERSON GROWTH

The growth building block comprises all of the individual opportunities and support that people get along their path of professional *and personal* growth within the organization and without. Yeah, it's a big block.

To cultivate whole-person growth, we've seen some leaders work with each of their direct reports to set a quarterly personal goal that has nothing to do with work itself, but is something that the person (not just "the worker") wants to do. Maybe it's running a marathon or taking a watercolor class. We asked one of our clients who did this what his experience was. He found that not only were his coworkers into the idea of sharing and documenting a personal goal, but these goals also provided an opportunity for them to connect over and talk about nonwork parts of their lives. Instead of asking how work was going, they could check in on their training or painting. It wasn't distracting or taking time away from work talk; it added to their understanding of each other and helped build trust between them. We've also worked with leaders who implemented growth plans focused on "what's next" to help people think about where and how they want their careers to grow. Sure, this might mean that person eventually leaves the role they're currently in, but how awesome is it if you, as their leader, can help people achieve bigger goals and reach their stretch opportunities? That *should* be what you want; leadership success is best measured by how successful your people go on to be.

For leaders, fostering a whole-human approach to growth can be foreign. You might perceive your domain as work and, more specifically, the current work scenario (i.e., you as leader and your direct report as an employee). Anything outside of that, while possibly great for building a friendship, isn't part of the job. But all people want to grow and are thinking about how they can best do that. Individuals are always asking: *Where do I want to be in five or ten years? What are the skills that I want to lean into? What do I want to do next? Who do I want to be and become?* As a leader, you have an amazing opportunity to take a guiding role in connecting employees' now to their next, their role and strengths to where they want to go. How great would it be to say, "I can help. I can help support you in your personal goals. And then also see how that might fit into the organization as you grow and evolve."

EXPERT TIP:

EMPLOYEES INDICATE THAT FEELING RESPECTED IS
THE MOST IMPORTANT ASPECT OF WORK CULTURE

In a language analysis of 1.4 million Glassdoor reviews that
employees wrote about their employers, researchers at MIT Sloan
School of Management found that the feeling of being respected
at work is 17.9 times more powerful a predictor of culture score
than the typical topic. They share, "Respect is nearly 18 times as
important as the typical feature in our model in predicting a company's overall culture rating, and almost twice as important as the
second most predictive factor, supportive leadership."[2] Respect is
not only *more* important, it is far and away *the most* important.

MENTORSHIP

 **INDIVIDUAL**

Have you ever thought about all the different ways people can teach others
within an organization? A seasoned team member teaching a new hire is
a common scenario, but there are so many other ways that we can teach
and learn. We can teach up and across, too. A strong culture will enable,
welcome, and encourage that because no matter who you are or what roles
you play, there is always something new you can learn (it's that growth
mindset concept again!). And, every person has expertise or perspective
they can teach others. Everyone has things to learn and also to share. That
is the type of mentoring we build into work cultures: everyone throughout
the company openly shares knowledge and experiences for the betterment
of all, no matter their position, tenure, or role. When you, and an entire

organization, embrace mentorship, it primes you for growth and opportunity. On an individual level, a mentorship mindset allows people to admit that they don't know everything (always true) and empowers them to share what they know (always desired). That simply makes everyone smarter.

Aside from creating a smarter work environment, a mentorship mindset shuts down information hoarding, which we all know creates obstacles and roadblocks and is a huge drag on organizations. The core reasons for information hoarding vary: people's egos, fear of becoming irrelevant, a belief that teaching takes too much time, an individual clinging to the belief that they're the only one smart enough for a particular task, and on and on. When you create a cultural norm around sharing expertise and knowledge and reward that behavior, information hoarders will become freer with information. They will have to if they want to stay relevant. Employee transitions—when someone leaves the organization or changes roles—often reveal the pain of knowledge hoarding and the pricelessness of information sharing. If Joel in accounting retires without passing on his institutional knowledge, his team will be left scrambling. But if Joel spends his last three years mentoring and sharing his knowledge, the team will be in a much better spot.

A 2018 study by Panopto, a video software company, found staggering support for the value of embedding information sharing into your organization. Included in "Workplace Knowledge and Productivity Report" were the following findings:

- Respondents believe that 42% of their knowledge is unique to them and their experience, not standard, role-based knowledge. That means nearly half of any given employee's knowledge base can't be found in a book or training manual; it's in their heads and learned from experience.

- 81% of respondents said "personal & work experience" was the hardest type of knowledge to replace when bringing new people onto a team (compared to "professional training" at 11% and "formal education" at 8%). So that 42% of people's knowledge that is unique to them is highly valued by others and difficult to replace.

- On a weekly basis, people spend an average of five hours waiting on others for information and six hours duplicating efforts that they know are already happening but don't have access to.

Mentorship and knowledge sharing also save organizations money. "We find that by preserving and sharing knowledge, smaller enterprise-size businesses might save as much as $2 million in employee productivity, while larger firms could save upwards of $200 million or more."[3] This underscores that all people have unique, valuable information that their colleagues want to learn or have access to because having that knowledge would improve their productivity.

Despite these findings, this open-sharing way of approaching mentorship can create tension. It goes against how many people view expertise and information ownership. Some people feel better when they believe they're the only ones who know something—it makes them more secure. If you experience pushback to such mentoring, Table 9.A shows a few quick comebacks to the resistance.

TABLE 9.A. RESPONDING TO PUSHBACK ON KNOWLEDGE SHARING

COMPLAINT	RESPONSE
"It takes too long to teach someone else."	"You should be able to mentor and share information in ten-minute-or-less time frames. We're not talking about lectures on SharePoint folder structures. It's simply conveying bite-size pieces of your wisdom to people around you."

"It took me a long time to master this; I don't want to show it to someone else."	"What are you afraid of? Really? You will still know the information. You don't lose your mastery when you help others develop their own. If you see an opportunity to mentor someone, it's your responsibility to do it."
"I don't have anything else to learn."	"Is it that you know everything or are afraid of what you don't know? Growth is an expectation here, so you must find a way to create that opportunity for yourself."

In the end, it's fulfilling to both teach and learn. It creates collaborative opportunities and intellectual networks that pay off financially (as shown above) but also emotionally. We all know that no one has gotten to where they are on their own. When you can enable those connections within your organization, you can help individuals grow and thrive and increase group intelligence—work smarter, not harder!

PERSONAL WHY

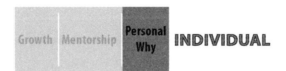

As a leader, one of the most powerful forces you can help people unleash is their personal why, what gets them out of bed every day. It gives them motivation, purpose, and fulfillment in their work and their lives. When we can apply even some of that *why* to our work, we can often go further and commit more energy to tasks or projects because we connect with the outcome, or bigger-picture context, on a personal level.

Every role and every person has a why. There is no role too minor or too simple for a deeper purpose. And every person has something that gives them energy. Finding where the role and the person can intersect is the sweet spot every leader should be looking for. And yes, sometimes we have to look for it. We aren't all changing the world in our day-to-day jobs. We can't all be doing a job that entirely overlaps with our personal why, but that doesn't mean we can't find something in our work, in some small way, that we can connect with on a deeper level.

A real power boost comes when as a leader, you can connect an individual's personal why with their role's why, and then connect all that to the organization's why. For example, one of our employees at Keystone sees the following connections between the three levels of *why*:

- Personal Why—to ignite the belief in people so that they can do, and be, more than they ever thought possible

- Role Why—to sell and execute services to growth-minded leaders/companies to help them grow as individuals to be impactful leaders, creating a positive culture and scaling the organization in a fun, healthy, and sustainable way

- Organization Why—to drive impact at a *human* level

If people feel a great pride in their personal purpose, understanding how that purpose informs and contributes to their role, and understanding how their role directly impacts and reflects the organization's why, you have total alignment. Of course, the purposes won't line up exactly, but exploring them can uncover unexpected connections and makes the effort worthwhile.

Most leaders we work with have never had a conversation with their team or their direct reports about their whys. When digging into purpose in the article "Help Your Employees Find Purpose—Or Watch Them Leave," the authors at McKinsey & Company wrote, "Our research found that 70 percent of employees said that their sense of purpose is defined by their work. So, like it or not, as a company leader, you play an important part in helping your employees find their purpose and live it."[4] There is a bit of a discovery process because most people haven't even articulated their own whys. Still, there are ways to access this to help people and yourself as a leader utilize the *why*. Try asking questions such as the following:

- Among the jobs or roles you've been most passionate about, is there a through line?
- What is the most fulfilling part of your current role?
- What do you get fired up about?
- What could you imagine doing for no money and why?

Because our *why* is the core of who we are and signifies what we believe in, tapping into it leads to high levels of sustained well-being and performance.

PEOPLE AS INDIVIDUALS

As we've said all along, organizations today are acknowledging that everything they do (or don't do) is because of people—and not just people in the collective sense, but people as individuals who live full lives and have interests both inside and outside of work. Your responsibility is to make sure that you nurture your organization's greatest asset by providing growth opportunities, mentorship to foster continuous learning, and help for individuals to understand how their personal contributions fit into the broader picture of the organization.

CHAPTER 10

Your Culture from the Outside In

*"It takes twenty years to build a reputation
and five minutes to ruin it."*

—WARREN BUFFETT

FIGURE 10.1. The external-level building blocks from the Impact Model

C ulture does not stop at your door. There is a back-and-forth between what happens inside and outside your walls. When your employees are out in the world having dinner, going to networking events, or meeting with prospective clients, your culture—and how they speak about it—is on display. And how people outside the walls perceive your brand and their experience with your organization impacts the people at your workplace. Imagine if every time you shared your organization's name in a conversation, people reacted with an "ewww" face because they heard that it was a terrible place through people and news stories. In that case, it would be hard to go to work every day and give your best effort—that negativity would nag at you. The constant influence and flux of these internal and external factors on people also ultimately impact your culture.

BRAND

Great organizations understand their brand and culture must align with each other. Culture is where your brand is born. Your brand is an expression of your culture and is created from the inside out: the behaviors that people and the organization exhibit create an impression that becomes your brand. And how that brand is perceived, the reputation you have internally and externally, and the authenticity of that brand expression will drive retention and engagement among employees, and loyalty and ambassadorship among customers. In the article "Align Your Brand With Purpose, Inside And Out," marketing and branding expert Fran Biderman-Gross shares, "As marketing has changed over the years, it's become clear that we must look inward as well as outward. As today's world values authenticity, companies should take every opportunity to go beyond the external. If you want to overcome any marketing challenge, what you say to the world outside must be in alignment with how you think and act, publicly and privately."[1]

This alignment can help employees, too: Your brand can reinforce cultural expectations as a form of accountability. It's easy to see when an employee is not being "on brand" and when they are, which enables people to point it out to get behaviors back on the right course. Here are some examples of how a brand you present to the public can play out internally:

- A customer service representative who always complains about customers and is not responsive to their questions would be "off brand" in a company that has a value and a brand of being customer solutions focused, always wanting to find the right solution that serves the customer.

- A company likes to advertise that in its culture, people value each other and everyone's unique skills and contributions. An "on-brand" leader will regularly engage with employees to understand and recognize individuals skills; they will focus on further developing and maximizing employee strengths by giving them more responsibilities that align with their strengths and removing what they can that is draining to the employee/does not align with their strengths. An "off-brand" leader sticks to rigid interpretations of job responsibilities, taking a one-size-fits-all approach rather than allowing for different interests and capabilities.

Ultimately, your brand is the value proposition to work for and do business with your organization. What is the value of being associated with your organization? Are there negative consequences or reputational dangers in being affiliated with the organization as either an employee or a vocal customer? Take Amazon, for example. If you live in a community that champions "buy local," you won't win any friends by aligning with Amazon. But if you live in a community that wants to attract the many jobs created by having a local Amazon warehouse, then alignment may bring benefits.

If your brand is associated with negative or unpopular sentiments, or if it is disingenuous, your internal culture will suffer. If your brand is robust and consistent, your culture will be positively impacted and informed by it. When your brand and culture are aligned, you will have clear, confident, strategic marketing that attracts your target market and a strong employment brand that attracts people who can be positive contributors to your culture.

As you think about your brand in relationship with your culture, consider the following issues:

ARE YOUR BRAND AND CULTURE ALIGNED?

Your brand and culture inform each other and can directly influence how everyone "lives" the culture. In "Build a Culture to Match Your Brand," brand positioning expert Denise Lee Yohn writes, "If your company culture is aligned and integrated with [your brand] identity, your employees are more likely to make decisions and take actions that deliver on your brand promise."[2] Alignment will reinforce each one and demonstrate that you're authentic. If there is misalignment, the inauthenticity will erode any positive efforts you make. For example, if your marketing brand touts innovation and creativity as your core DNA but your internal culture is top down and punitive, no amount of branding can cover up the reality of your culture.

WHAT ARE PEOPLE SAYING ABOUT YOUR ORGANIZATION?

Every employee and customer is a walking billboard for your brand.

Employees walk around representing your brand's quality, integrity, and feeling. If they say negative or defeated things during happy hours, what will all those people think? Conversely, how great will that sound if they rave about how many opportunities they're getting in their role? So, you want to make sure that all the other dimensions of your culture are solid, or your employees will be out in the world representing some not-so-great aspects of your organization.

Customers who identify with your brand will amplify it. If you're an industry disruptor, your most enthusiastic customers will likely be people who embrace forward-thinking innovations. If you're a local legacy manufacturing company, your customers may embrace loyalty and community. You want that external reputation to align with how you talk about your organization and the culture you're building.

ARE YOUR CONSUMER BRAND AND
YOUR EMPLOYMENT BRAND CONSISTENT?

If your organization has a marketing brand that underscores honesty and security, but your culture doesn't allow or encourage truth telling as a practice, your brand and culture are misaligned. This can cause disjointed experiences as potential employees are researching your organization and for clients or customers who want to do business with an organization that genuinely reflects their value, in this case honesty.

DOES YOUR BRAND ATTRACT PEOPLE WHO
THRIVE AT YOUR WORKPLACE AND WHO
HELP YOUR WORKPLACE THRIVE?

A strong brand makes a huge difference in who even considers working at your organization and who stays on board once they're there. Because most people don't want to just clock in to make a paycheck; they want their own purpose and values to align with wherever they spend about eight hours each day. If the word on the street is that your culture is cutthroat, competitive, and constantly in "code red," you're going to attract people who enjoy the feeling of working at a place like that and put off people who don't enjoy that. If your culture is known as flexible and inclusive with high expectations for excellence, you will attract people who align themselves with those qualities. And if, somehow, your culture shifts from one to the other, you will lose people along the way.

A positive internal and external brand is crucial for maximizing your culture and fostering a high-impact environment. Internally, people will feel good about their role in something they're proud to represent, and externally, you will have the reputation and trust from customers to keep growing.

CUSTOMER EXPERIENCE

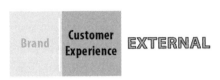

We're often asked, "Are customers actually impacted by our culture?" At times, people ask out of genuine curiosity, but more so it's a question skeptics pose because they want to poke holes in our belief that culture—especially a negative one—will always impact your bottom line. They're really trying to say, "No one outside an organization cares about or knows if our culture is crap, so why are we investing in it?" If you have engaged and empowered employees who find value in their work and feel valued in return, they will be infinitely more invested in building a positive customer experience. There is no greater incentive for creating satisfied customers than satisfied employees.

A 2020 whitepaper published in conjunction with a study conducted by *Forbes* and Salesforce shared that 70% of executives agree that improved employee experience (EX) leads to improved customer experience (CX), which in turn leads to rapid revenue growth. In fact, companies that have both high EX and CX see almost double the revenue growth as those that do not.[3] Similarly, a 2021 survey of 655 IT decision makers conducted by IDC (International Data Corporation) titled "Relating Employee Experience to Customer Experience" found "85% of respondents to the IDC survey mentioned above agree that an improved employee experience and higher employee engagement translate to a better customer experience, higher customer satisfaction, and higher revenues for their organization."[4]

Customer experience tells you how engaged and satisfied your customers are regarding their interactions with employees at every level of the organization. We've found that if an organization has poor customer experience scores or reviews, the root cause can be found in the culture. If there aren't systems and processes that efficiently get your customers what they need—the product they purchased or the service they subscribed to—their experience suffers. If intentional communication isn't happening between teams, the delivery team may not know orders were canceled and will try to deliver them. If employees are not held accountable to the organization's cultural expectations, then core processes can falter, which can lead to poor customer experience. If innovation isn't going on, your customers' needs may slowly begin to go unmet, and they will take their business elsewhere.

Like your employment brand, if your cultural building blocks are not stacked squarely and securely, your customer experience will suffer. Have you ever called a customer service line and been met with a drab, distracted voice that is barely interested in helping you? It isn't pleasant, right? You want to get your question answered or your order fixed, but it's like pulling teeth and, frankly, sucks the energy out of you more than a typical transaction. This experience is the result of a culture problem. Something about that employee's experience in their role at that organization is either leading them to act that way or allowing them to act that way. For example:

- Their shift may be too long with no added benefits for pulling a double shift, so they think they don't matter to the organization.

- They may not know how their career can grow at the company, so they think they have a dead-end job.

- They may not have had the training or mentoring to learn how to build their skills, so they feel insecure or ill-equipped to take action.

- They may have observed ways to improve a process related to their job but were not allowed to share it because of their rank, so they feel demoralized.

- They may not know the value that their individual conversations with customers help the overall trajectory of the organization.

- They may not trust that when they put in a refund order that it will get approved, so they think their efforts are worthless.

- They've never met or had meetings with their team leaders, so they don't feel connected to or part of a team.

If an employee has thoughts like this about their experience, it will impact their actions and interactions every moment of every day, and there is no way to keep the impact of that within your walls. Customers and clients will feel it. If employees feel scared, unmotivated, unsure, or unprepared, it's evident in all kinds of ways. When employees feel good about their job, have positive thoughts about their workplace, and have a strong relationship with their manager or supervisor, their actions and interactions will be more positive.

A strong culture helps employees understand their *role* in customer experience and helps them understand the customer experience *itself*. Continuing on the phone call theme from above, have you ever been on the receiving end of a pissed-off customer call—the kind where they're raising their voice and saying explicitly demeaning things? I think we've all had this experience, and it's terrible. Your culture will be what rescues people from terrible morale or empowers them to do something about that experience. Do you have a "make it right" culture that enables people to fix whatever needs fixing, or do you have an elaborate approval process that requires employees to jump through hoops to help anyone? Are you logging customer complaints but not doing anything to uncover and fix the repetitive issues? The customer experience team should be sharing feedback with the team to understand how it aligns with purpose and goals, as well as trends on issues and customer needs. These frontline observations can be game changing for how the rest of the organization responds to and empathizes with customers, which can further fuel employees' engagement in creating better solutions. See, it's all interconnected!

If you're making it hard for people to help or are not doing anything with customer dissatisfaction, your employee engagement will suffer greatly. A robust and customer-centered culture draws out one of humans' most natural instincts: to help. We *want* to solve a problem that someone is experiencing. We *want* to be the hero for an hour or a minute. Create a culture that allows people to flourish, and people will, in fact, flourish.

YOU ARE NOT ALONE

Your organization, like every other organization, does not exist in a vacuum. You have employees, customers, and other stakeholders who are part of the communities in which they live. Your business and all these stakeholders benefit from what these communities provide—and you *will* have an impact on the community, hopefully for the better, not the worse. It is a reciprocal relationship: how well you manage all the interconnections in the ecosystem containing your business will determine whether your culture can thrive, and how you manage your culture will influence whether those interconnections help your business thrive.

PART III

Taking Your First Next Steps

By now, hopefully, we have made the case for culture and you're a believer. You can see the connection between culture and impact. You understand how a strong culture is built on and made up of a foundation of strategy, conscious leaders, and empowered people. And you think there are some ways you and your organization could get better, which may mean increased revenue or profits, being more productive, making your people a little happier and more satisfied, or some other impact.

So, now what? Now that you are armed with this knowledge, how do you take the building blocks and start building a better and more impactful culture? You can start **now** by taking the four steps we cover in the next chapters:

- Collecting data to assess where you are today, your **base camp** (chapter 11)
- Defining where you want to go (chapter 12)
- Mapping a path forward (chapter 13)
- Tracking the progress you make (chapter 14)

We end the section with some final tips on dos and don'ts as you start this journey (chapter 15).

Beyond what you'll find in this book, we've developed an entire website—www.thecultureclimb.com—dedicated to supporting you through your Culture Climb. It has resources, articles, and the tools we share in the next few pages, all of which are available for free. Think of the site like a coach in website form—we wanted to provide as much as we could to get you as far as you can on your own.

CHAPTER 11

Establish Base Camp

"The journey of a thousand miles begins with just one step."

—LAO TZU

GOAL: Figure out how your culture measures up right now, at the start of the climb

TOOL: Culture Check-up

OUTCOME: A more objective measurement of what building blocks are strong and which ones need some attention

---

"That's not an issue here," "People are really happy with [*our values, how we communicate, our professional growth plans, etc.*]," or "We know exactly what we need to work on."

We hear comments like this from people all the time. And being the curious people we are, we always ask, "But how do you know? And do you *really* know exactly what your people think of your culture right now?" Most leaders assume a lot about their culture. This happens for various reasons, few of which are bad; it's simply how most organizations have managed their culture over the years. And we see two primary scenarios when leadership teams make assumptions.

First is the all-too-confident team: the leaders think they know what is best for their organization. For example, suppose a company decides to review its rewards and benefits program because the leadership believe it could be more competitive. They form a committee, the committee reviews different program options, meets with different providers and experts, and comes back with a set of recommendations. Then the leadership team chooses one of the recommendations that, while more expensive, offers the level of premium options that they believe will set a new standard for their industry. They excitedly roll it out at a staff meeting . . . and the tenor in the room isn't what they expected. No one was nearly as excited about the new program as leadership thought they'd be. What happened? The leadership assumed people valued something that they didn't (or not as much as the leadership team valued it), and they assumed that the change would increase employee satisfaction. Yet what they discovered, after all their work, was that the organization's rewards and benefits program wasn't actually a problem or at least it wasn't so bad that making improvements was a priority for employees. So the company ends up wasting resources and not creating the intended impact. Has your company made changes to "improve culture" that went over like a lead balloon? Would you like to avoid this kind of costly mistake?

The second reaction is having a company on autopilot mode—they keep making similar choices to ones they've always made, keep using the same logic they always have because it seems to be working well enough, or they simply don't stop to ask, "What could we do differently?" This makes total sense. Humans are wired to do what's comfortable and familiar; we're inclined to find the path of least resistance because it's efficient for us. But that is a risky approach in a work environment because it's also how to get left behind. No organization, or leadership team, can rest on its laurels.

The solution to both of these scenarios is to proactively assess your culture so you'll know exactly what your employees value, what you can leave as is for now, and where you have to go off autopilot. Having a clear understanding of your culture prior to making changes is vital because when it comes to the effort you put into your culture, it's not the *amount* of effort you put in that makes a difference, it's *how* you direct that effort. In "Return on Culture: Proving the Connection between Culture and Profit," Erica O'Malley, organizational strategy partner at Grant Thornton, observes, "The 69% of companies that don't measure culture are still spending money on culture initiatives they feel are valuable to their employees. My suggestion to them: stop spending money until you know whether it's paying off." For example, the "Return on Culture" study showed a significant discrepancy in what executives believe about their physical workplace and what employees believe about it: 57% of executives believe a pleasing workplace environment is critical to employee loyalty, whereas only 36% of employees believe the same thing.[1] What you and the rest of your organization believe and want may not line up. Real, authentic awareness is the gift that measuring gives you, which is crucial for thoughtful leadership and for impactful organizations.

It can be easy to nod along while reading about the importance or the value of matters like mentorship and personal whys, but it's another to think critically about what these areas mean for the organization and the other humans, including you, in the organization—and whether those concepts are alive and well in your employee experience.

Determining where your organization is strong and where it needs improvement requires humility and careful observation. Understandably, we all want to see the best versions of ourselves and our organizations. But this is the time to take a deep breath, remove the rose-colored glasses, look directly at the behaviors you see around you, and be honest about what they say about the culture as a whole.

- Are the values being actively used to make business decisions?

- Does the behavior you see around the office feel inclusive, and do you witness people feeling safe enough to offer differing opinions in discussions?

- Do your job candidates align with the level of expertise and skill your organization needs, or do you struggle to attract quality candidates?

While these are not the actual questions on the assessment, you can see that the act of reflecting on your actual culture, not your aspirational culture, requires vulnerability—and conscious leadership. Let us assure you: It's okay that what you observe may not be perfect. It doesn't mean you or others have failed—all organizations have some behaviors that represent a strong and positive culture and some that don't. Your honesty, combined with the objectivity of taking an assessment, is important. Without both, you may end up inaccurately patting yourself on the back for something that isn't true.

The tool described in this chapter—the Culture Check-up—will help you understand what is really going on in your company as you begin your Culture Climb. How your culture measures up today is your baseline against which you can compare all future improvements. A baseline is an important data set because as you decide how to enhance your culture, your baseline gives you a meaningful measure of what's strong, what's fine, and what could use improvement, and it also helps you celebrate progress along the way. Even more importantly, getting a clear picture about your culture today provides a new perspective, or a more objective perspective, to take on your climb with more clarity and more confidence.

GATHERING DATA USING THE CULTURE CHECK-UP

THE CULTURE CHECK-UP CAN HELP YOU:

- Gather objective information about your culture relative to the building blocks defined in the Impact Model

- Provide data that will help you prioritize your Culture Climb efforts

The Culture Check-up assessment is a survey form that you can download from the Culture Climb website. You can give it to as many people as you like, and ask each one to rate how effective your organization is at each of the building blocks. For people who have read this book, completing the Culture Check-up will help them connect what they've read to what they experience in their organization—but reading this book is *not* a prerequisite!

The complete assessment is too detailed to include here, but Table 11.A shows an excerpt with statements related to the organizational level of the Impact Model. As you can see, people are asked to rate how closely your organization currently comes to the ideal using the following scale:

- *1 – We don't do this at all*
- *3 –* We *talk about it, but we don't do it well*
- *5 – This is our superpower*

TABLE 11.A. THE ORGANIZATIONAL LAYER OF THE CULTURE CHECK-UP ASSESSMENT TOOL

BUILDING BLOCK	DESCRIPTION OF WHAT GREAT LOOKS LIKE	RATING
Accountability	GREAT organizations set clear expectations and have consistent follow-through with responsibilities and tasks for individuals, teams, and departments. Leaders hold themselves and their teams accountable, and peers hold each other accountable.	1
		2
		3
		4
		5
Systems and Process	GREAT organizations operate on a business framework made up of subsystems and processes that allow them to consistently hit their goals and results. The framework enhances clarity to the business objectives, creates an effective communication cadence, decreases errors, improves customer and employee experience, and promotes consistency across the organization.	1
		2
		3
		4
		5

BUILDING BLOCK	DESCRIPTION OF WHAT GREAT LOOKS LIKE	RATING
Social Impact	GREAT organizations believe in a social contract with their surrounding communities. They view giving back and doing business in an ethical, sustainable, inclusive, and health-promoting way for the employees, community, and society. Their social impact efforts attract and engage employees, boosting organizational profits and productivity.	1
		2
		3
		4
		5
Innovation	GREAT organizations believe innovation is a growth mindset and not an event. They are given the opportunity, time, and creative space to bring forward ideas or solutions that add value to the organization or customer. Innovation is a requirement to stay relevant and consists of asking the right questions to generate the right ideas.	1
		2
		3
		4
		5
Collaboration	GREAT cultures create the conditions for collaboration. Both teamwork and collaboration bring employees together to achieve the same goal. To achieve effective collaboration among employees, the team must be aligned and open to fully welcome and adapt to each member's skills and knowledge for better decision-making.	1
		2
		3
		4
		5

In the full questionnaire, there are twenty statements, one for each building block in the model. So the ideal score would be 100 points (a rating of 5 for all twenty statements).

For best results, have people beyond the leadership team complete the Culture Check-up. It is tempting to ask only an inner circle, perhaps just the leadership team or a selection of managers. We understand, and it is okay to start there, but it's better to extend the assessment to as many people in the organization as possible to get a complete and accurate picture. Ideally, you have a diverse set of people take the Culture Check-up—different tenures, roles, teams, and even locations (if that applies to your organization). Because culture is everyone's responsibility and everyone contributes to it, you will get far better data if you include people throughout the business. This is hard, and it's not how many leaders or leadership teams like to operate. Yet, without listening to all the voices, you might be fooling yourself about the actual status of your culture.

EXPERT TIP:

CONSIDER REAL-WORLD EXAMPLES WHEN RATING CULTURE

As people try to answer the assessment honestly, encourage them to think about actual examples of behaviors as they review each statement. For example, when thinking about the Clarity of Vision building block, people should ask themselves:

- Have I ever witnessed people using our organization's vision to make decisions?
- As we shared the vision in our last all-staff meeting, what were people's facial expressions—bored, perplexed, excited?
- Have prospective employees ever commented, in a positive or negative way, about the vision and direction we're headed?

You're more likely to get out of your gut and into reality by conjuring real-world scenarios.

ANALYZING THE CULTURE CHECK-UP RESULTS

Once all your participants have completed the Culture Check-up evaluation, you will need to compile and analyze the results. For any individual or as an average of all respondents, the overall scoring can be interpreted as follows (remember, the highest possible total score on a single assessment is 100):

- **20–40: Inconsistent** – Cultural behaviors are inconsistent, and it's hard for you to be effective and optimized in that environment.

- **40–60: Informed** – Behaviors may still be inconsistent, but you're aware that things could be better and you want to improve them.

- **60–80: Intentional** – You are proactively engaged and working on your culture, clear on what you want to change and are taking steps to make those changes.

- **80–100: Conscious** – You have reached a level of familiarity with how to work on your culture, and it's embedded into what you do as an organization.

While the overall scoring gives you a general sense of direction, you will need more granularity to identify where you should focus your efforts. You can do this by determining an average score for each building block and creating a list or diagram that shows the ratings for each building block. For example, here is an example of the average ratings for the team level of building blocks:

- People Development = 3.5

- Innovation = 2.2

- FUN! = 4.3

- Collaboration = 4.0

Alternatively, you can develop a visual depiction of the results, like the example shown in Figure 11.1.

FIGURE 11.1. Visual depiction of Culture Check-up results

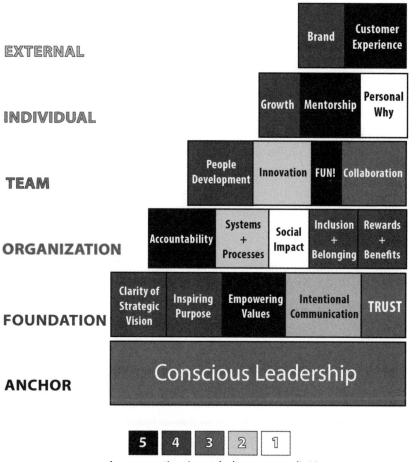

EXTERNAL

| Brand | Customer Experience |

INDIVIDUAL

| Growth | Mentorship | Personal Why |

TEAM

| People Development | Innovation | FUN! | Collaboration |

ORGANIZATION

| Accountability | Systems + Processes | Social Impact | Inclusion + Belonging | Rewards + Benefits |

FOUNDATION

| Clarity of Strategic Vision | Inspiring Purpose | Empowering Values | Intentional Communication | TRUST |

ANCHOR

Conscious Leadership

5 4 3 2 1
Average rating (rounded to nearest digit)

This company realized overall it was doing fairly well in twelve of the twenty building blocks (rated 4 to 5 on average) but has some work to do in the other eight blocks (rated 1, 2, or 3 on average).

INTERPRETING THE CULTURE CHECK-UP RESULTS

Once you receive the report, your leadership team should spend some time reviewing and discussing the results. This is the cold-hard-look-in-the-mirror time. Sounds like a really fun meeting, right? Exploring all the ways you could be better? We know it sounds rough, but it can be an invigorating experience if you allow it. The beauty is in knowing what is true right now about your culture. With this, you have more clarity and the power to make great changes.

If you and other respondents were honest, the scores in your report will show a range. If it shows your responses were all great or all below average, retake the assessment—neither of those outcomes are accurate. The truth is, every organization has room for improvement. Sometimes it's hard to believe that about other companies; looking from the outside in, you might assume they've got it all figured out. But no leadership team or organization ever has it all figured out because culture is constantly evolving. Given that it's never constant, it's also never perfect—it can be strong, resilient, and positive, but never perfect.

The process we recommend is the following:

1. Review all the total scores. Where do people think you fall generally in the "inconsistent" to "conscious" scale?

2. Identify all the building blocks where the average score is 3 or lower. These are your opportunities for improvement (back to that growth mindset again!). You're building an intentional culture to discover how to make more impact—and your low scores are your starting points for deeper inquiry and guideposts for making a plan. Where are you missing the mark and potentially not supporting the culture you want?

3. Identify all the building blocks where you scored 4 or higher on average. Don't just focus on the negative! Celebrate the wins, too. You want to know what you have in place that is working well? Where does your culture really shine? This is important for sustainability.

Not only will it remind you of what you're already great at, but it can also help keep those building blocks strong. Think about our climbing metaphor again: when you're on that steep hill, it pays off to pause, turn around, and enjoy the view. Sure, you still have a climb ahead, but you have also accomplished part of your journey. Take that in and celebrate it.

4. Discuss the results thoroughly. You want to ask many questions. It's tempting to say, "We got low scores in X, Y, and Z, so let's invest there." That may be true, but the report as a whole is a portrait and may offer more information the more you examine it. Some example questions to ask are the following:

    ° Are our low or high scores clustered in a particular area?

    ° Where should we focus our energy?

    ° Are there discrepancies between the way leadership sees the organizational culture and how teams and employees see it?

    ° Are we as strong as we think we are?

    ° Are the perceptions we have about our culture accurate?

    ° Are there any surprises?

    ° Were there any building blocks we never address or take action on as an organization?

    ° Are there patterns in either the highest or lowest scores? For example, if all the team blocks received low scores, you may want to think about how teams are organized and managed. If all the growth and innovation scores are low, you may want to examine if fear and risk aversion negatively impact people's experiences.

    ° Are there any connections between the extreme scores—the highs or the lows?

    ° Which of the building blocks—positive or negative—are related to the priorities in our business strategy?

  ° After the discussion, select **three to five building blocks (at most!)** that will be your priorities for the next year. These should feed into your Culture Map (see next chapter), where you identify specific steps you can take.

Your experience with the Culture Check-up and the time you spend making observations will help you determine your next steps from a place of understanding and perspective. It gives you data to be aware and informed about right now so you can move into your next stage with intention.

EXPERT TIP:

PREPARE FOR CHANGE

Culture will always change. Every new input can influence the thoughts, actions, and interactions of the people in an organization. For example, new hires, industry disruptions, local political events or news, developments among your competitors, and economic trends all impact how people feel about their environments and how they act and react. Moreover, these inputs can change what people want, need, and expect from their workplace. Of course, no one can prevent these changes, but you can prepare for the fact that the culture will change, and you will need to respond to the change. In part, that's why it's important to measure your culture regularly—this will allow you to detect small changes before they become massive pivots.

BOLSTERING YOUR BASE CAMP

Doing the Culture Check-up and evaluating the results are the most critical actions you can take on your way to improvement. Simply by engaging with the questions and thinking critically about your culture, you will become more aware, and so will anyone else who does the assessment. You will start to notice the way people are acting at work and think about what they tell you about your culture—you will likely start to even change some of your own behaviors.

Going forward, you will get even more from the Culture Check-up if you take the time to do it annually. Then, you will be able to monitor and measure progress on your efforts and spot natural changes as they unfold. Because culture is constantly ebbing and flowing, it's important to keep a pulse on your people, the dynamics in the workplace, and how your organization is keeping up with all the dimensions that keep your culture strong. Each time you go through the exercise, you will get more data, gain more insights, and have additional practice navigating the always-changing cultural water.

CHAPTER 12

Set Your Compass

"It's not about perfect, it's about effort."

—JILLIAN MICHAELS

GOAL: Define how you want your culture to look and feel in the future

TOOL: Culture Compass

OUTCOME: A clear picture of what you want your culture to evolve into

---

You've completed the Culture Check-up and studied the Culture Report, so you're ready to start taking action, right? Not so fast. Before your leadership team decides what to do, you need to know *where you want to go*. Only by knowing the destination can you make good decisions about what changes can help you get where you need to be. And this is where the Culture Compass will help.

THE CULTURE COMPASS VISION STATEMENT
THE CULTURE COMPASS WILL HELP YOU ANSWER:

- How do we paint a compelling and inspiring picture of the culture we want to have now and as we grow into the future?
- What do we need to do to make the changes?
- What behaviors will we expect from people in our new culture that we don't have now?

The Culture Compass is a creative and strategic tool that will define the culture you want today and into the future—it's a key part to operationalizing and mobilizing your desired culture. The Culture Compass will answer, "Where is the company going and what are the ways that I as an individual can start shaping my thoughts, actions, and interactions to help us grow into our future state?"

The tool has three parts:

> **1.** BACKGROUND ON WHAT INFORMATION YOU SHOULD CONSIDER AS YOU BEGIN TO THINK ABOUT YOUR FUTURE CULTURE

Background information to collect for a Culture Compass statement:

1. Leverage your core values. You can refer to your company core values to help describe the vision for your culture. These are a driving force behind your culture and determine how people think, act, and interact in your business.

2. Review your purpose (or mission) statement. It will be important to consider the overarching goal of your company and how you

envision achieving it. Your purpose/vision statement gives meaning and purpose to your company culture.

3.   Consider your employees. Think about your current and ideal employees and how you would describe them. Your culture is a living aspect of your organization as a result of the people on your team. Think about their unique characteristics and how they communicate and work together to achieve results.

2. PROMPTS TO HELP YOU SHAPE THE VISION OF THIS FUTURE CULTURE

Prompts for developing a Culture Compass statement:
With one or all three of these things in mind, use the following prompts to help you write a description of your ideal culture.

Our company culture will feel like _____
_____.

Our company culture will promote _____
_____.

Our company culture will celebrate _____
_____.

Describe how you want people to think about and perform work:

Describe how you want people to communicate and work together:

Describe how you want the work environment to add value to employees and teams:

Words that best describe our company culture: circle your top 3 and then narrow down to #1.

Connected	Motivating	Respectful
Casual	Inclusive	Trustful
Fun	Challenging	Welcoming
Collaborative	Relaxed	Nimble
Transparent	Empathetic	Fast paced
Nurturing	Rewarding	Positive
Progressive	Engaging	Family
Autonomous	Curious	Integrity

3. SPACE TO DRAFT A CULTURE
COMPASS VISION STATEMENT

Space for writing your Culture Compass vision statement:

Now write a paragraph describing your ideal workplace culture.

There are different methods you can use to get to the vision statement. Sometimes the leadership team will take on the task. Others will assign the task to a committee or team that is responsible for presenting a draft statement back to the leadership team. We've found it helpful to include the marketing team or someone on the team who has a strength with writing who is assigned to develop a draft vision statement for others to review.

In a way, the Culture Compass mirrors some of the foundational building blocks. Like a clear vision and an inspiring purpose, a well-defined Culture Compass vision statement will help you and the people at the organization understand where you're headed. You will build trust and buy-in by sharing what you hope for as an organization. The Culture Compass doesn't replace any of your foundational efforts, but the act of creating and communicating a consistent and collective destination is incredibly impactful.

ARTICULATING YOUR FUTURE ORGANIZATION

To make the most impact, get specific about defining the culture your organization needs to thrive. Articulate how people and teams behave in your strengthened culture:

- What are people thinking, feeling, and doing?
- What conditions are supporting the people in this new environment?
- What achievements or learnings will you be promoting or celebrating?

For example, one workplace might celebrate the agility to pivot their product offering to meet an unexpected turn in the market. In contrast, another organization may promote its ability to collaborate meaningfully and transparently with new clients. The first culture might feel faster paced, while the second might feel more nurturing. Neither is better and, hopefully, each version serves the business and other needs of the people within the organization.

Expressing these details will help you develop a clearer picture of the culture you want to create. Despite how it sounds, creating a bold, specific description of your ideal culture doesn't have to be grand. In fact, it should be grounded enough for people to relate to (or not) and see themselves in (or not). Here are three examples of Culture Compass vision statements from different organizations to get you thinking about your own:

Our philosophy continues to be that we approach every relationship with honesty and integrity. Moreover, our focus remains on the people we are helping, not just the problems we are solving.

What we value most is working with talented people in highly creative and productive ways. Our people-first approach allows us to be more flexible, creative, and successful in everything we do.

Our culture celebrates, supports, and trusts our teammates and their unique talents as we evolve together. We are an inclusive team who believes individuals' passions collectively drive our purpose.

These statements share specific and unique characteristics that describe what it's like to be at the workplace and suggest how people might act and contribute within those environments. In the first, there is a distinct sense of mutual respect and humanity. In the second, there are elements of innovation and adaptability. The third evokes images of collaboration and creativity. As you're reading them, you can imagine behaviors that are consistent with these visions and how you would or would not fit into the environments. That's exactly what you want with your own statement.

FINE-TUNING YOUR COMPASS

Before finalizing your Culture Compass, pressure test it! Compare the vision statement to your values and purpose—they should all be consistent in the behaviors they are inspiring. For example:

- Suppose a company has a value of "Do what's right, not what's easy." Imagine how people enact that and how you would know people are truly living and breathing that value. In this case, their Culture Compass may use words like "patience," "long view," or "support" to encourage behaviors that allow for "right" decisions, not just easy ones.

- Another company has a purpose of improving postsecondary education in rural areas. They would want to think about the qualities that the people and work environment must have to fulfill that purpose day in and day out and be fueled by it. Their Culture Compass might underscore empathy or problem-solving to steer people toward behaviors that help overcome challenges.

The more robust the picture you paint in your Culture Compass, the easier it will be to establish goals and pathways to make that picture a reality. A rich description helps you bring others along on your climb and gives structure to their own behaviors. Similar to your experience reading the paragraphs above, your Culture Compass will do the same as employees and prospective employees read it—they will envision themselves and determine how to act accordingly. Like the organizational vision, the Culture Compass will direct energy and attention so people's efforts aren't going in crisscrossing directions.

Culture is an all-hands effort, so how you share where you're headed and how you invite people from across the entire organization onto the journey directly impacts your success. Intentional communication about why this newly articulated culture is yours to own and the impact you hope it will have on the people and organization will help ground the ambiguous future state in meaning and purpose. The reality is that change, even positive change, can be difficult for people. They wonder, "What will this mean for me?"— that's human nature. Hopefully, what people hear in a well-defined Culture Compass will help them see ways in which their experience will be enhanced, even if they're unsure exactly how.

As you progress on your climb, review your Culture Compass every year. Doing an annual review allows you to gut check whether it's still right for your people and your organization. It might not change at all for a few years as you find your footing on your climb. Or, perhaps one part snaps into place quickly, but others take longer. That's all completely normal. It will likely take anywhere from one to three years to see a major change in your culture. That doesn't mean you have to wait that long to start seeing *any* results—you will get an immediate lift from the work you are doing now, but long-term change and long-term impact take time.

We can say from experience that the fact you're even reading this book, doing a Culture Check-up, talking about your results, and collectively setting a vision of how you want to grow puts you ahead already. Simply having culture conversations will raise awareness and will help all the leaders in the organization start seeing things a little differently—you may even feel an immediate shift. Putting time and investment into how people think and feel in your organization and what they want out of the workplace is a powerful exercise, which enhances performance by providing clear expectations on how work is to get done together. What you talk about is what you, and others, will focus on and pay attention to. And when you bring people along, they feel invested and believe their ideas and perspective matter—because they do. This work proves that to them!

EXPERT TIP:

BE PATIENT

Change takes time. You will see improvements as you start to intentionally build your new culture, but achieving your long-term vision fully will require sustained effort. Impatience or fatigue may creep in, and when it does, remember to focus on the small improvements and keep going. Most change happens in increments—there is no lightning flash when the teams go from siloed to collaborative work. It happens over weeks, months, and years as people adjust with small behaviors. But those small behaviors do eventually add up to something big.

AIM HIGH

Knowing the destination is the only way for your leaders to decide what actions will take you closer to the culture you need. While the building blocks of a positive culture are consistent (as defined in the Impact Model), the specific behaviors and experiences you cultivate at your organization within the building blocks will differ from those established as the workplace down the street or across the country. The exact effort that will lift you from "now" to "better" is all your own. There is no way to use benchmarks or templates to get you there. It's your culture, what your people want and are experiencing, the way your leaders and people think, act, and interact. That can't be compared to or sampled from another company. Aim for what **great** looks like in your organization and culture.

CHAPTER 13

Map Your Way Forward

"Action is the fundamental key to all success."
—PABLO PICASSO

GOAL: Focus on what you need to accomplish, and prioritize your next steps

TOOL: Culture Map

OUTCOME: Actionable steps to take this year to make progress on your goals

---

Your Base Camp helps you figure out where you are now. The Culture Compass helps you orient your future direction. Now, you can begin plotting out the route to take on your Culture Climb. This is where the rubber meets the road and you convert the information you've learned into decisions about what you can do *now* that will get you *where you want to be*. As you consider your big vision and how your culture could grow, the Culture Map will keep you focused and help you prioritize. It's what keeps your energy on what you *should and need* to do, not all the things you *could* do.

THE CULTURE MAP

THE CULTURE MAP WILL HELP YOU ANSWER:

- What is this information really telling us to focus on first?
- In what kind of time frame can we make healthy, sustainable changes?
- Who is responsible for the various milestones?

The Impact Map is a form that helps you document your decisions about where you want to be in one year as captured in two or three annual goals, and what you can do NOW (in the next ninety days) to achieve progress toward those goals. It has four parts, as shown in Figure 13.1:

- **Part 1**: What you need to do over the next year (an **annual goal**) to be successful in making progress toward your culture vision
- **Part 2**: How you will know if you successfully achieve the annual goal
- Part **3**: What building block(s) this goal supports
- Part **4**: What ninety-day actions you need to take to achieve each of the annual goals and who is responsible

TABLE 13.1. CULTURE MAP FORMAT

ANNUAL GOAL	
DESCRIPTION OF SUCCESS (WHAT YOU WILL SEE IF YOU ACHIEVE THE GOAL)	
BUILDING BLOCK THIS GOAL IS FOCUSED ON	

	ACTION	ACCOUNTABILITY
90-DAY ACTIONS TO ACHIEVE GOAL 1, AND WHO IS RESPONSIBLE	(A)	
	(B)	
	(C)	

You should complete this information for two to three annual goals.

This information will align everyone and give you actionable structure as you start the climb.

SELECTING PRIORITY GOALS

So where do you start? By reviewing the Impact Model and gathering the information and analysis you have done to date:

- Your Culture Base Camp—your analysis of the Culture Check-up, including your conclusions about what building blocks of the Impact Model you are strong in and where you are weak. While goals aren't always directly tied to building blocks, they do relate. Each goal should strengthen your weak blocks or reinforce mission-critical blocks. Because of this, it's important to identify the building blocks that you hope will be impacted by your goal.

- The Culture Compass vision statement you developed to described your desired future culture

Review this information and choose two to three goals that will help make that vision a reality. Use your Culture Base Camp *and* your Culture Compass vision statement to be realistic about your goals. The difference between them might be huge or small depending on where you're at as an organization. If your vision is all about amazing communication but your assessment showed that your organization is weak in intentional communication, this vision is going to take more effort. Whereas if your Culture Check-up showed that communication was generally strong but you want to be more intentional, the effort to achieve the vision will look different. Neither is bad, but your goals to achieve that vision and how long it may take to get there will depend on where you're at.

How do you choose what to focus on? Without a doubt, if your Culture Base Camp revealed weaknesses in any of the **foundational** building blocks, first set goals that will help you level up in those areas. Conscious leadership, a clear vision, empowering values, an inspiring purpose, intentional communication, and trust are prerequisites for any of the other aspects of culture. You can put some effort into strengthening other areas simultaneously, but do not skip the foundational blocks entirely. As the foundation strengthens, you will get stronger faster in the other blocks because they're crucial to the thoughts, actions, and interactions demonstrated in other parts of your culture.

Aside from focusing on your foundational opportunities, your goals can be any **specific and measurable action** that will either validate that your culture is what you think it is or help you make necessary improvements. You may not know if your actions will definitely improve exactly what you want to improve, but beginning to forge the path toward your future organization has to start somewhere. In all likelihood, any goals you set will generate action and attention on your culture, and that is a great initial outcome in itself.

Before you get overzealous, there's a reason we limit the annual goals to three. It's tempting to want to do more. More innovation? Yes! Better people development? That too! We also want a better vision and more communication, and let's build team trust! Of course, we all want to be strong in every building block—and you can get there—but if you take on too much at once, you risk achieving nothing. You can't change it all at once or your actions won't be authentic; you'll be scrambling and half-assing things, undermining your whole cause. Focus on your biggest pain points first and build from there, and remember, working to make your strengths even stronger is a meaningful action as well. So be incremental with goals, and keep them focused on the first next steps.

BE SPECIFIC ABOUT THE ANNUAL GOALS

The annual goals included on the Culture Map must be clear and specific. This helps everyone know if and when the goal is achieved. Some goals may have a quantifiable success metric, but others may be more qualitative. As you define your goals, play devil's advocate. Ask "what if . . . ?" and push the language to be as specific as possible—you essentially want the definition for success built into the definition of the goal.

For example, the two goals that follow are not clear:

- Create a community volunteer strategy.

- Implement a performance management process.

With each, you can imagine a few different outputs or outcomes that could technically achieve the goal. What you want is to add language so you get exactly what you need as an organization from the effort people are putting into the goals—whether that need is more data, an experiment, a new process, etc. Here are how those goals could be clarified to help create clearer expectations:

- Create a community volunteer strategy. → Create guidelines for our community volunteer program and hold two company-wide volunteer events.

- Implement a performance management process. → Define, document, and implement a performance management process, communicate and train both the managers and employees on the process, and ensure that 100% of employees have a performance review by the end of the year.

Because this is usually one of the most challenging parts of the process, here are a few other examples of clear goals:

- Create a three-month standard onboarding plan for all positions to ensure clarity and understanding of roles are achieved for new employees.

- Create and share the long-term vision of the organization, and ensure each department has goals aligned to the vision.

- Create and execute an employment brand strategy that improves our time to fill positions.

In the end, if you and your team can see the goal and all know exactly what outcome will happen on the "done" side of the goal, you're off to a great start.

Let's revisit the Culture Compass statements shared in chapter 12 to illustrate how your Culture Compass, goals, and building blocks may relate.

PRIORITY GOALS EXAMPLE 1

The first Culture Compass vision stated, "Our philosophy continues to be that we approach every relationship with honesty and integrity. Moreover, our focus remains on the people we are helping, not just the problems we are solving." To gain momentum on this vision, the organization may set the following annual goals:

- Develop a customer satisfaction survey that assesses our ability to connect with customers in developing a relationship based in trust.

- Create an organizational purpose statement and determine all the locations where it should standardly appear, and then develop a communication strategy to ensure clarity and understanding across the organization.

These each advance or reinforce some of the key attributes of the culture the organization mentions in their vision. The first will confirm they're achieving the outcome they want from honest relationships: authentic connection with people. And the second speaks to their interest in their humans doing the work, not just the work itself. Together these goals underscore and build trust, fueling the human side of their business.

PRIORITY GOALS EXAMPLE 2

The second Culture Compass statement declared, "What we value most is working with talented people in highly creative and productive ways. Our people-first approach allows us to be more flexible, creative, and successful in everything we do." For that, the organization may:

- Enhance the onboarding process to include a group experience that taps into the creative power of each cohort to advance a project or the overall business.

- Explore the feasibility for an on-site daycare service using an employee focus group to help steer the discovery.

The first goal builds toward and fosters creativity at a critical point in an employee's experience: the first thirty to sixty days. The type of onboarding it outlines could demonstrate that the organization walks the creativity walk (it's not just a word they throw around) and helps people tap into their own creative mindsets. The second goal shows a commitment to providing supportive flexibility. Moreover, it's clear that because they expect people to be productive, they are willing to create conditions to help them do it.

NINETY-DAY ACTIONS AND ACCOUNTABILITY

Once you determine your goals, the next step is to articulate specific actions you will take *in the next ninety days* to achieve them (you can call these quarterly goals, but they should be treated separately from fiscal quarters). These should be micro-steps that break down the annual goal into smaller increments, and they should be assigned to one person to drive the work through the finish line (accountability for the win!). This nesting nature of the vision, annual goals, and quarterly actions will help you sustain your efforts.

Breaking a big task down into smaller parts has many benefits. First, it allows you to make progress without being overwhelmed or overexcited about the big picture. Each smaller part, the ninety-day action, keeps you focused, for the short term, on a single task, while knowing it's contributing to long-term progress. Moreover, each phase allows you to see if you've moved the needle in the right direction, or whether you have to adjust your path. For example, if your first ninety-day action had unintended consequences that moved you further from your goal, yet the goal is still a worthy one, you can make a new plan. If you weren't doing the ninety-day actions you might have just kept forging ahead, not realizing you were not quite on the right path. And last, this approach helps you avoid bright-shiny-object syndrome. You have probably witnessed this in action, or maybe even fallen prey to it. It's when you're happily and productively working on a plan and then boom, some new idea comes out of nowhere, and off you go, pursuing it, which distracts you from your original plan. The effect of bright, shiny objects is often ad hoc actions that have no relation to each other or a broader goal—exactly what we're trying to stave off by connecting intentional actions with your desired vision.

EXAMPLE CULTURE MAP

Committed to emerging from the pandemic stronger than ever, the leadership team at a manufacturing company in the Midwest identified two priority annual goals: the first was to reduce costs by reducing waste and scrap, and the second was to reduce turnover (increase retention) by improving employee engagement. You can see their Culture Map in Figure 13.2, which describes the two goals and the immediate actions they will take to make progress toward those goals.

FIGURE 13.2. EXCERPTS FROM A CULTURE MAP

ANNUAL GOAL #1	REDUCE WASTE/SCRAP COSTS BY 10% (HELP CONTROL COSTS)
Description of success (what you will see if you achieve the goal)	Scrap and waste from top 5 production lines will be down 10% by March 15 of next year

ANNUAL GOAL #1	REDUCE WASTE/SCRAP COSTS BY 10% (HELP CONTROL COSTS)	
Building block this goal is focused on	Systems + Processes	
90-day actions to achieve goal 1, and who is responsible	ACTION	ACCOUNTABILITY
	(A) Gather data on current scrap/waste over 2-month period	Luella M, operations manager
	(B) Analyze data to look for trends (shifts, products, suppliers, etc.)	Keith from Data Support
	(C) Develop plan for improvement	Luella M, operations manager

ANNUAL GOAL #2	IMPROVE EMPLOYEE ENGAGEMENT AND RETENTION
Description of success (what you will see if you achieve the goal)	Raise engagement ratings from survey by 3 points (from avg of 4 to at least avg of 7 on a 10-point scale) Turnover down by 50%
Building block this goal is focused on	Inclusion + Belonging; Collaboration

ANNUAL GOAL #2	IMPROVE EMPLOYEE ENGAGEMENT AND RETENTION	
90-day actions to achieve goal 2, and who is responsible	ACTION	ACCOUNTABILITY
	(A) Hold focus groups to get more details on poor ratings from Culture Check-up	Jack L, HR manager
	(B) Share data with leadership team	Jack L, HR Manager
	(C) Develop plan to improve engagement	Renee B, COO

CREATE LIVING GOALS

Since the Culture Map asks you to identify *annual* goals but *quarterly* (new ninety-day) actions, you need to review the Culture Map quarterly to set new actions for the quarter ahead. While reviewing, confirm that the goals still make sense and the description of success still holds up. As you go, you might find that you've overshot your annual goal because quarterly actions are going slower than you thought. No worries—this is all part of the process. Simply adjust and keep moving. In the end, some forward momentum is what you want, and it's what will get the organization to that next, stronger version of itself.

EXPERT TIP:

PRACTICE ACCOUNTABILITY

Each quarterly action must be assigned to one person and only one person. That means no matter what, that person is account-able for it—they may delegate tasks, but they are still on the hook for it getting done. And, depending on how you scored in account-ability on your Culture Check-up, this may be your first exercise in practicing greater accountability. Don't let the opportunity to lead by example pass you by. Have potentially uncomfort-able conversations if a quarterly action doesn't get completed. Accountability doesn't mean things are done perfectly, without issues, 100% of the time. It means the person sees a commitment through, even if it is bumpy, imperfect, or late, and manages all the consequences of their actions. Be attentive and intentional with how you hold people accountable at this stage or you may set a bad precedent.

CHAPTER 14

Track Your Progress

"Progress is made where progress is measured."
—JACK LALANNE

GOAL: Track how your culture efforts have had an impact on your overall business

TOOL: Culture Scorecard

OUTCOME: Documented metrics that show if and how the business is improving

---

I f culture is the key to making more impact as an organization, you want to measure organizational-level growth as well as culture growth, right? Yes! So once your Impact Map is in action, tracking intentional metrics will help you know how your efforts and investment are impacting your business. While your annual Culture Check-up will help you diagnose issues and decide which levers to pull within your culture specifically, your scorecard will tell you if what you're doing is making a difference in the larger business picture.

Tracking critical business outcomes is how you will determine the ROI of your culture efforts, which is how you will know if your chosen areas of focus are worthwhile. A meaningful scorecard is achievable and rewarding once you figure it out. Finding the right metrics, however, is one of the most challenging aspects of this work. Yes, we saved the hardest for last. Metrics are difficult for a few reasons:

- First, like culture, the combination of metrics that tell you that your business is impactful in the way you want it to be will be entirely unique to you and the impact you are hoping to make at the current moment.

- Second, the relationship between the specific parts of culture and specific business outcomes isn't a one-to-one relationship. You won't work on your innovation building block and then see a direct correlation to an increase in sales or customer satisfaction. And yet, there *will* be a cause and effect because the actions and behaviors that shift as you solidify and build your culture will also shift outcomes.

Your scorecard needs to change as your culture and organization grow and evolve. What you measure each year or few years should reflect your future-state destination. Asking, "Are these the metrics that will tell us that we are on track for where we want to be in three to five years?" is a constant question to be asking yourself and your team.

You can think of your scorecard as a helpful quarterly complement to your annual Culture Check-up. With a quarterly scorecard, you will get quick quantitative feedback about your efforts, which allows you to make incremental changes as you take your climb. If you see growth or improvements in your numbers, great! That tells you you're on the right track. If you're investing in culture and seeing no difference in your metrics, then you may not be investing in or cultivating your culture in the right ways. Stagnant or declining metrics will tell you that an initiative or change didn't have the effect you expected. Finding the right combination of efforts and outcomes will take some time. It's not realistic to have all the right answers about your culture and your impact right away. In fact, it often takes anywhere from six months to a year of tracking to figure out if the numbers are indicators of what you need to know.

THE CULTURE SCORECARD

THE CULTURE SCORECARD WILL HELP YOU DOCUMENT:

- What business metrics are most important for us to get a pulse on our business?

- How can we know, and show others, that the investments we're making in culture are paying off?

- Where and how is our business improving because of the culture work we are doing?

As the label implies, the Culture Scorecard helps you keep track of how well you're doing compared to your goals and desired outcomes. The format of the Culture Scorecard (see Figure 14.1) is very simple on purpose, allowing one to quickly review the metrics you have identified, the baseline performance you will establish at the start of your efforts, and how it changes (or not) over time.

CULTURE IMPACT METRIC	TARGET	MONTH 1	MONTH 2	MONTH 3	...

FIGURE 14.1. Format of the Culture Scorecard

CHOOSING WHAT TO TRACK

Imagine you could know nothing else about your business except five to six metrics, and those alone informed every decision you made about your culture for the next six months to a year. You couldn't talk to anyone, you couldn't check in on clients or projects, and you didn't even see your monthly or quarterly finances. What would those five or six metrics be? What data would give you specific enough information about your business to tell you the intelligent next steps? Your answer should be the beginning of your scorecard.

Identify a set of leading indicators that make the most sense for your business and how you want to grow or evolve. Consider the different aspects like operations, finance, employee experience, and customer experience. Within each of these business areas, find indicators that tell you if your business is healthy and your culture is creating the type of relationships and outcomes you're hoping for.

To help you get started, here is a list of example metrics that demonstrate progress for developing a stronger overall culture:

- Voluntary Resignations

- Terminations

- Open Positions

- Filled Positions

- % Quarterly Reviews Completed

- # of Employees with Development Plans

- # Employees on Performance Improvement Plans

- ENPS – Employee Net Promoter Score

- Employee Satisfaction

- Performance Reviews: Percent Goal Achievement

- Number of Employee Referrals

- Engagement Response Rates/Scores

- Production Utilization Rates

- # of Reported Injuries

- Customer Satisfaction/NPS

- Customer Complaints

- Errors

- Backlog

Other metrics could include gross profit margins, new products launched, customer complaints, average products per customer, average tenure of employees, EBITDA, budget versus actuals, average product launch, utilization rates, repeat customers, and customer referrals.

There are hundreds of business metrics to draw from, so choose metrics that help you know if you're moving toward the better, stronger version of your organization. What does your impact look like in numbers?

Which of these you choose (or others you may have identified) varies from company to company. For example, Figures 14.2 and 14.3 show two examples of metrics selected by two different companies, as captured in their Culture Scorecards:

FIGURE 14.2. COMPANY "A" CULTURE SCORECARD

CULTURE IMPACT METRIC	TARGET	MONTH 1	MONTH 2	MONTH 3
EMPLOYEE EXPERIENCE: 6-MONTH RETENTION RATE	Up from 50% to 65%			

CULTURE IMPACT METRIC	TARGET	MONTH 1	MONTH 2	MONTH 3
EMPLOYEE EXPERIENCE: INDIVIDUAL GROWTH PLANS IN PLACE	50% of employees have them in 3 months			
BUSINESS PERFORMANCE: CLOSED DEALS	Improve by 15 percentage points by end of fiscal year			
CUSTOMER EXPERIENCE: ERROR RATES	Reduce from 5 per encounter to ≤1			

FIGURE 14.3. COMPANY "B" CULTURE SCORECARD

CULTURE IMPACT METRIC	TARGET	MONTH 1	MONTH 2	MONTH 3
EMPLOYEE EXPERIENCE: EMPLOYEE REFERRALS	Double by end of year			
FINANCE: PROFITABILITY BY SERVICE LINE	All service lines up 10% by end of year			

OPERATIONS: EFFICIENCY RATIOS (EXPENSES/ REVENUE)	Improve by 15 percentage points by end of fiscal year			
CUSTOMER EXPERIENCE: AVERAGE CUSTOMER VALUE	Reduce from 5 per encounter to ≤1			

BEST PRACTICES FOR CULTURE SCORECARDS

The purpose of your scorecard is to get a pulse on whether you're making progress toward your definition of healthy culture. You should be able to say with clarity why you choose each metric, what it tells you about your business, and what that tells you about your journey to getting better. To those goals, follow these tips:

GET GRANULAR

Broad metrics are not good for helping you decide if your culture efforts are achieving what you want them to achieve. You might have to choose granular metrics. For example, "revenue" is a possible metric, but what would you be able to decipher from that broad number? More revenue is not a bad outcome, of course, but the goal of a scorecard is to know whether you're taking steps in the right direction, so your metrics should give you feedback about the actual efforts you're making. Rather than total revenue, perhaps it's a type of revenue or an acquisition method (email sign-ups versus cold calls). Getting more specific gives you more details and awareness, and it allows you to more easily assess what's truly going on.

DEFINE AND DOCUMENT GOALS FOR EACH METRIC

There is no way to benchmark your culture against other organizations: 30% turnover may be great for one company and terrifyingly horrific for another. What is most important is that you and your team know exactly what progress looks like for your situation—your growth, the culture you're striving for, and all the needs within your organization. Before you start measuring over time, document a baseline for your metrics now, and determine what a healthy outcome would be—your goals. With this, your measures over time will have context, and you'll have criteria against which to compare your quarterly numbers.

EXPERT TIP:

IDENTIFY YOUR OWN CADENCE

Best practice is to review your metrics on a monthly basis, but you can decide the right cadence based on the measures you select.

OBSERVE YOUR REACTIONS TO THE SCORECARD

If you review your scorecard and you find yourself and the team glazing over the numbers, that indicates that you might not have found the metrics that accurately give you a pulse on the business. If you find yourself or hear others saying, "Oh, it's okay if that metric hasn't moved . . ." or you make excuses for why a number hasn't budged, you probably haven't articulated your most impactful metrics.

While it's not a hard and fast rule, good metrics generally inspire a conversation. They will make you curious and ask questions like, "Why did that change? How can we understand that more? What is happening there that we need to dig into?" When an important metric is off or when it improves, it should spark an immediate reaction because you know that movement—for better or worse—is something worth understanding.

USING THE SCORECARD TO MOTIVATE

Over time, the scorecard will give the pulse of your organization and can be a powerful motivational tool—we all like to know that what we're doing is making a difference. By wrangling your random culture efforts into a Culture Compass for direction, an Impact Map for focus and prioritization, and a fine-tuned scorecard, you'll know if you're getting the results you need to justify and validate your culture investment. You'll start to eliminate the busywork of ad hoc attempts that you hope move the needle—make people more engaged, increase productivity, etc.—and start to be able to say, "Yes this is working and worth our time" or "Nope, we still have some tweaking to do." And with that information you can see if and how you're going from good to great.

EXPERT TIP:

USE A COACH

When you're stuck or hit a plateau, call an objective third-party coach. Of course, we'd love for you to call us, but any culture coach can help. Objective insight is often needed after you start your climb. It's truly difficult for insiders to see their teams and culture with clear eyes, as much as they may want to. Organizational habits can be as embedded as personal habits, and after awhile, we just stop seeing them. Finding the right metrics can be tricky; sometimes you need an expert eye. Bringing someone in from the outside can illuminate the "this is just how we do things" habits and inject new ideas into your problem-solving.

CHAPTER 15

Embarking on Your Journey

"How you do anything is how you do everything."

—T. HARV EKER

Hey! You've made it through the why, what, and how of the Culture Climb! Now we want to leave you with a few critical best practices to stick in your back pocket as you embark on the journey. If you're too excited and want to jump straight to action, go for it, and come back to this section when you're stuck or want to level up.

COMMUNICATION WILL MAKE OR BREAK YOUR EFFORTS

All the energy you put into understanding, assessing, and envisioning your culture, and all the effort you put into your map to make improvements, will be for naught if you don't also invest time and careful thinking into communicating it with every single person in your organization. You know that advice, "Say something seven times in seven ways for people to truly hear, understand, and remember"? When it comes to communicating culture changes, we couldn't agree more.

Attitudes will shift the minute you share that the organization is doing something new, like the Culture Climb. And while you might be really excited about your bright future, most people struggle with change, even when it's "good" change. Empathize with that and draw on your best communication skills to help employees see that going from now to next is not threatening. Here are some guidelines for thinking about what you should communicate to make sure people understand the goals and rollout of your change efforts.

THE WHAT AND THE WHY

Transparency is a quality you see in most healthy, successful organizations. What you choose to share will tell people, directly or indirectly, how much you want them to care or to be involved. If you only communicate a few high-level talking points, they'll assume the rest is none of their business, or fill in the blanks with their assumptions. And when it comes to culture, what's going on is everyone's business. What should you share with people in your organization?

Project

The project-level communication is about the big picture: where you're going and how to get there. It's the road map that will help people see above the day-to-day details and into the organization's future state. This communication should be inspiring and purposeful.

Progress

Communication about progress helps people feel part of the journey. Don't be afraid to share mistakes or pitfalls along the way—these will highlight that culture and working on culture are an organic process, and continue to build trust. On the flip side, don't shy away from celebrating every win, accomplishment, or goal met. We all need positive reinforcement, and these celebrations will rejuvenate people, especially those doing the work.

Perspective

Communication doesn't always have to be factual; it can be personal. For example, perhaps each manager shares what most excited them about the culture vision or what they learned from taking the Culture Check-up. This shared approach to messaging underscores the "everyone is responsible for culture" point. It also helps put more nuance and subtleties to the messages because each person will phrase things in their own way. Hopefully, individuals will be able to see themselves and their perspectives reflected in them.

Including the "why" behind every business decision is so important when it comes to conversations about your culture, especially as it's evolving or as you're growing. This connects the heady goals with the heart behind your effort. You're embarking on your culture journey to make more impact, and that is a powerful thread you can weave into the way you talk about what you're doing. When you connect the purpose to every task or ask, people can truly understand the endgame and believe in the work—and if they believe in it, they take action toward it.

THE WHO

Culture efforts are all-hands-on-deck projects. Therefore, you have to consider all the ways you can make the project relevant for all people. Think about the layers and parts of your organization and how you are giving people within those layers context about what's changing and why. Consider how messages are shared with:

The Whole Organization

How are the story of your culture journey, the road map of what you're doing, and the progress being shared in all-company settings? These collective experiences can ensure people hear the same things in the same way and at the same time, and rally people together behind a big idea.

Teams

How are the culture efforts shared at the team level? Managers and directors should lead the effort to translate and model the purpose of the culture work at the team level. They are in a great position to underscore how the efforts will positively influence the team and to inspire teamwork by finding ways the team can work together toward the culture vision or a team goal that reflects the culture vision. Team-level discussions are opportunities to consider existing dynamics and share ideas about making the organizational work more relevant to the team's work.

Individuals

How are managers following up with individuals about the organizational efforts to ensure every person's questions or concerns are addressed? Make sure managers are proactively making space for conversations about the changes that are happening. These direct relationships or one-on-one meetings may be when employees feel the most comfortable asking questions or voicing opinions. And for managers, these personal conversations are an opportunity to help individuals understand how they contribute to the culture efforts. Directly inviting people to participate in the work forges a deeper commitment to the goals on their part. Once they know how they fit into the overall goal and what their place is within it, they can more easily buy into the journey.

AND THE WHEN

It's a big mistake to come out of the gate strong with an all-hands meeting, share a big vision with lots of energy, to only then retreat to your office, start doing the work, and not speak about the culture outside of your team for another year. When this happens, no one outside of the people involved in the day-to-day plans or actions has any idea how changes are going. The silence and lack of transparency send a message in and of itself, which can lead to all kinds of problems like apathy or resistance. Establish a communication cadence that aligns with the tools you're using and the goal of keeping everyone informed and excited about the efforts:

Annually

Culture Check-ups are done annually, so the results should be shared out annually as well. If people know you're doing the work but never see or hear evidence, you may inadvertently foster distrust or disbelief in the process.

Quarterly

Share the updated Impact Map when you define new ninety-day (quarterly) actions. Discuss any changes to the Impact Map—progress on the previous ninety-day goals and new goals being established—and comment on what unfolded over the previous quarter. Emphasize any metrics that you track monthly or quarterly so people can see any improvements that you made (yay!). This furthers the feeling that people are on the journey with you.

Monthly or Weekly

Depending on your work cycles, find ways to share bits of progress or points of view between the big informational check-ins. There are myriad ways to loop people in to the concept of culture and get them thinking about their own culture contributions. Above, we suggest managers share their perspectives. You could have a Q&A or an Ask Me Anything (AMA). You could share short content, like articles or videos, about individual building block concepts. You could choose a rotating topic that highlights your organization's foundational building blocks—so perhaps one value a month. You don't have to overdo it, but the more culture is on people's minds, the more they will be personally aware of how they can impact it.

Organically

Consider how you can filter all regular internal communication through a culture lens to add heart to what might otherwise be pretty straightforward messages. For example, if you're sending a message from the president or CEO, review it through a cultural lens: Does it have the tone and feel of the culture you're cultivating? Are the organizational values upheld and evident in how it's shared or what it states? Is the purpose being used to underscore what's being said? Every piece of internal messaging—every email, announcement, intranet page, and presentation—represents your culture. Think of these as internal marketing moments when you can really emphasize the cultural attributes you want to instill throughout the organization.

There is no silver bullet for how you communicate, but you must do it as intentionally as possible in ways that make sense for your values, your organization, and your people. Also, when in doubt, assume more is always better.

CULTURE IS A MARATHON, NOT A SPRINT

Sustainability is important for cultural change. The reality is that you will always be working on your culture because it's a living, breathing part of your organization—it's never done. As people come and go, as your market shifts, or as society changes, your culture will respond. So don't think about perfection or speed as evidence that you're doing it right. As we've said, the fact that you're paying any attention at all to your culture means you're already doing the most challenging part.

In the end, you want to be the tortoise, not the hare, in your approach. Take time, reflect, and be swift and decisive when you have to, but recognize that consistency is more important than immediacy. When you work on one aspect of the culture authentically and intentionally (i.e., probably slower than you would like), it builds trust within the organization that the culture changes are being taken seriously. Whereas if you're trying to do fifty things at once, your efforts may not resonate in the same way. So a careful and thoughtful approach actually strengthens trust—the cornerstone of culture—as you go!

BE PATIENT WITH THE CYCLES

On the road to culture change, there are phases. You can be in one phase one year and either revert or catapult to a different phase the next year. We sketch out the phases as the following:

- **Initial inconsistency**—This is often where organizations are when they start their climb. When cultural behaviors are inconsistent, people are all doing their own thing. These behaviors aren't necessarily bad or harming your organization. It's just hard for you to be effective and optimized in that environment.

- **Informed**—In this phase, behaviors may still be inconsistent, but you're aware that things could be better, and you want to improve them. You're tuned in to the fact that working on your culture could help make the organization stronger, even if you don't quite know what the right work is.

- **Intentional**—This phase is when you're proactively engaged and working on your culture. You're clear on what you want to change and are taking steps to make those changes. Moreover, you're measuring and assessing along the way to ensure things are moving in the right direction.

- **Iterative improvement**—After you've reached a level of familiarity with how to work on your culture, you may find yourself in the interactive improvement phase. This is when major evolutions have already happened, and now you're into the tinker-to-optimize actions.

You will cycle through all of these stages at different times along your journey. It's not going backward; it's simply the process of adapting to change. One year you might be totally intentional and consistent. Then an external factor influences the organization, and you're back at the informed stage while you assess the impact of that factor and how the organization can adjust. Then you may get intentional again and even maximize your impact for a while. But then the CEO leaves and the culture takes a hit and

behaviors are inconsistent. While it may be frustrating, you can always keep
leveling up, and dropping "back" is simply part of the climb.

FOCUS ON THE ROOTS

Remember that saying we share earlier in the book about "stop mowing
dandelions"? It's a waste of time to keep attacking the superficial symptoms
of problems; you need to dig down to the root causes. It's important to keep
that idea in mind as you look more objectively at your culture. We want our
culture model and the Culture Base Camp to help you diagnose problems
beneath the surface so you can figure out how to accelerate your impact.
But you have to commit to going there, asking deeper questions about your
culture and organization, and leading the changes that need to happen.

As you work on your culture, you will also have to work on yourself.
Indra Nooyi, former chairperson and CEO of PepsiCo has said, "If you
want to improve the organization, you have to improve yourself, and the
organization gets pulled up with you." Your thoughts, actions, and interactions must grow and adapt. The practice of asking deeper questions
and reflecting on what's really going on may be new behaviors for you.
Leaders are used to knowing things! We're smart! We are in charge for a
reason! But don't fool yourself with your own answers. Always ask yourself, "Are we actually getting to the root of our problems and addressing
them, or are we just skimming the surface because that's easier—are we
just mowing dandelions?"

CULTURE HAPPENS "WITH" PEOPLE NOT "TO" THEM

You build a culture *with* people; you can't achieve change by simply telling
them how you want the culture to be. You talk with people about the evolution and growth opportunities and invite them along. The most significant
culture change will happen when it's collective and nonhierarchical. That
doesn't mean you have to become Zappos or embrace holacracy as a business

practice, but when it comes to your culture efforts, always bring different people together from all parts of the organization to make it collaborative.

CAST A WIDE NET

After leadership gets on board and feels confident about the culture work, open the door to people who know the most about whatever topic you're addressing. We had a construction company client who made improved safety an annual goal. As they were articulating the goal and identifying quarterly actions, the leadership team kept hemming and hawing about how to actually meet the goal and identify the tasks that needed to be done. They just weren't entirely sure what improved safety would look like or where a lack of safety was currently an issue. And that's not a surprise: the leaders on the team were from the corporate side of the company, not on the ground and, like all of us, their perspective was limited by their experience.

We proposed they bring in people from the field to lead the charge to improve safety. If anyone knows about the biggest safety hazards and how incidents happen, it's the people actually doing the work. The shift to bringing other people from the organization into the leadership team discussion wasn't natural for them, but they tried it, and the minute the broader team clicked, they got excited. Immediately, safety became the most important goal for the year. The leaders *knew* the effort would have a significant impact because it was collaborative, informed, and directly affected everyday operations. At that moment, they realized that culture is interactive, not instructional: it was collaborative decisions leading to action, not simply leaders telling employees what to do.

You will always be learning different pathways or strategies for improving culture. Use the people around you, draw on their expertise and experience, and value their contributions. We know that the "with" not "to" approach can be challenging for leaders who came up in the ranks during the command-and-control style of corporate leadership. At every turn, it's important to revisit the values and practices of conscious leadership to stay present, humble, and curious about every development and detail that comes up. Being attentive to how your actions will drive or derail the climb is vital as all the parts are set into motion. A "with" approach will get you more—more momentum, more excitement, and more impact.

IT'S TIME TO START YOUR CLIMB

We hope that the practical steps here in part III as well as the information we share throughout the book have inspired you to launch a culture change effort in your organization. The hardest part of the climb is the decision to start. The next hardest part is *beginning* the climb—the first steps may feel awkward, but we've gotten overwhelming feedback from clients that even having conversations about the building blocks in the Impact Model leads to valuable insights about what's working and not working, and helps to align leaders around where the most impact can be made. Those conversations can motivate leadership teams to turn the sometimes soft and intangible topic of culture into clear actions linked to specific goals that can produce results.

You don't have to know all of the answers and solutions to start. Being willing to have the conversation and being open to improving is the most important factor to creating real change in your organization. As the business environment continues to change at a rapid pace, know that your investment in the Culture Climb can be the competitive advantage that your organization deserves.

Isn't that what we all want at the end of the day? Be the change . . .

"A positive culture is a place where people leave our organization each day better than when they arrived."

—JAIME TAETS

Notes

CHAPTER 1: THE CULTURE GAP AT WORK

1. Boris Groysberg, Jeremiah Lee, Jesse Price, and J. Yo-Jud Cheng, "The Leader's Guide to Corporate Culture," *Harvard Business Review*, January–February 2018, https://hbr.org/2018/01/the-leaders-guide-to-corporate-culture.

2. Carolyn Dewar and Reed Doucette, "Culture: 4 keys to why it matters," March 27, 2018, https://www.mckinsey.com/business-functions/people-and-organizational-performance/our-insights/the-organization-blog/culture-4-keys-to-why-it-matters.

3. Indeed Editorial Team, "What Is Work Culture?" February 22, 2021, https://www.indeed.com/career-advice/career-development/work-culture.

4. "The Business Case for Culture," Eagle Hill Consulting, accessed June 6, 2022, https://www.eaglehillconsulting.com/wp-content/uploads/Eagle-Hill-Consulting-Business-Case-For-Culture.pdf.

5. Donald Sull, Charles Sull, and Ben Zweig, "Toxic Culture Is Driving the Great Resignation," *MIT Sloan Management Review*, January 11, 2022, https://sloanreview.mit.edu/article/toxic-culture-is-driving-the-great-resignation/.

CHAPTER 2: SIX TRUTHS THAT BUST COMMON CULTURE MYTHS

1. Holacracy, holacracy.org, accessed August 20, 2022, https://www.holacracy.org/.

2. "Culture," Reed Hastings, accessed June 6, 2022, https://www.slideshare.net/reed2001/culture-1798664.

3. Denise Lee Yohn, "Culture Is Everyone's Responsibility," *Harvard Business Review*, February 8, 2021, https://hbr.org/2021/02/company-culture-is-everyones-responsibility.

4. Catherine Yoshimoto and Ed Frauenheim, "The Best Companies to Work For Are Beating the Market," *Fortune*, February 27, 2018, https://fortune.com/2018/02/27/the-best-companies-to-work-for-are-beating-the-market/.

5. Simon Sinek, *The Infinite Game* (New York: Portfolio, 2019).

CHAPTER 4: CULTURE AS FUEL: WHY THE CLIMB IS WORTH IT

1. Jacob Morgan, "Why the Millions We Spend on Employee Engagement Buy Us So Little," *Harvard Business Review*, March 10, 2017, https://hbr.org/2017/03/why-the-millions-we-spend-on-employee-engagement-buy-us-so-little.

2. Morgan, "Millions We Spend on Employee Engagement."

3. Morgan, "Millions We Spend on Employee Engagement."

4. "The Business Case for a High Trust Culture," Great Places to Work, accessed June 6, 2022, https://www.greatplacetowork.ca/images/reports/Business_Case_for_High_Trust_Culture.pdf, page 6.

5. Catherine Yoshimoto, "Great Places to Work are Great Performers," *FTSE Russell*, March 27, 2018, https://www.ftserussell.com/blogs/great-places-work-are-great-performers.

6. "Return on Culture: Proving the Connection between Culture and Profit," Oxford Economics, accessed June 7, 2022, https://www.oxfordeconomics.com/resource/return-on-culture-proving-the-connection-between-culture-and-profit/.

7. "The Business Case for a High Trust Culture," Great Places to Work, accessed June 6, 2022, https://www.greatplacetowork.ca/images/reports/Business_Case_for_High_Trust_Culture.pdf, page 15.

8. Nate Dvorak and Ryan Pendell, "Culture Wins By Getting the Most Out of People," Gallup, July 31, 2018, https://www.gallup.com/workplace/238052/culture-wins-getting-people.aspx.

9. "What People Want" report, Hays, accessed June 6, 2022, https://www.hays.com/resources/what-people-want-2017.

10. James K. Harter, Frank L. Schmidt, Sangeeta Agrawal, Anthony Blue, Stephanie K. Plowman, Patrick Josh, and Jim Asplund, "The Relationship between Engagement at Work and Organizational Outcomes," Gallup, October 2020,

https://media-01.imu.nl/storage/happyholics.com/6345/gallup-2020-q12-meta-analysis.pdf.

11. James K. Harter, Frank L. Schmidt, Sangeeta Agrawal, Stephanie K. Plowman, Anthony Blue, "The Relationship between Engagement at Work and Organizational Outcomes," Gallup, April 2016, https://www.gallup.com/services/191558/q12-meta-analysis-ninth-edition-2016.aspx.

CHAPTER 5: CULTURE IS YOUR JOB

1. Aaron De Smet, Bonnie Dowling, Marino Mugayar-Baldocchi, and Bill Schaninger, "'Great Attrition' or 'Great Attraction'? The Choice is Yours," *McKinsey Quarterly*, September 8, 2022, https://www.mckinsey.com/business-functions/people-and-organizational-performance/our-insights/great-attrition-or-great-attraction-the-choice-is-yours.

2. Alex Edmans, "The Social Responsibility of Business," filmed at TEDxLondonBusinessSchool, London, video, 17:25, https://www.youtube.com/watch?v=Z5KZhm19EO0.

3. "The High Cost of a Toxic Workplace Culture," SHRM, accessed June 6, 2022, https://pmq.shrm.org/wp-content/uploads/2020/07/SHRM-Culture-Report_2019-1.pdf.

CHAPTER 6: THE ANCHOR AND FOUNDATION OF A VIBRANT CULTURE

1. Mark Lipton, "Demystifying the Development of an Organizational Vision," *MIT Sloan Management Review*, July 15, 1996, https://sloanreview.mit.edu/article/demystifying-the-development-of-an-organizational-vision/.

2. Naina Dhingra, Andrew Samo, Bill Schaninger, and Matt Schrimper, "Help Your Employees Find Purpose—Or Watch Them Leave," *McKinsey Quarterly*, April 5, 2021, https://www.mckinsey.com/business-functions/people-and-organizational-performance/our-insights/help-your-employees-find-purpose-or-watch-them-leave.

3. Michael Mankins and Eric Garten, *Time, Talent, Energy: Overcome Organizational Drag & Unleash Your Team's Productive Power* (Brighton, MA: Harvard Business Review Press, 2017), 19.

4. Patrick M. Lencioni, "Make Your Values Mean Something," *Harvard Business Review*, July 2002, 5–9.

5. "The Culture Effect: Why A Positive Workplace Culture Is The New Currency," SHRM, accessed June 7, 2022, https://www.shrm.org/hr-today/trends-and-forecasting/research-and-surveys/documents/2021%20culture%20refresh%20report.pdf.

6. The team at Slack, "Trust, Tools and Teamwork: What Workers Want," *Slack*, October 3, 2018, https://slack.com/blog/transformation/trust-tools-and-teamwork-what-workers-want.

7. "Trust," *OED Online*, Oxford University Press, accessed March 24, 2022, https://www.oed.com/view/Entry/207004?rskey=WBer6Z&result=1&isAdvanced=false.

8. Amy C. Edmondson, "Psychological Safety, Trust, and Learning in Organizations: A Group-Level Lens," in *Trust and Distrust in Organizations: Dilemmas and Approaches*, eds. Roderick M. Kramer & Karen S. Cook (New York, NY: Russell Sage Foundation, 2004), 239–272.

9. Paul J. Zak, "The Neuroscience of Trust," *Harvard Business Review*, January–February 2017, https://hbr.org/2017/01/the-neuroscience-of-trust.

CHAPTER 7: THE ORGANIZATION

1. Daniel Pink, Drive: *The Surprising Truth About What Motivates Us* (New York, NY: Riverhead Books, 2011).

2. "Civic Life Today: The State Of U.S. Civic Engagement" report, Points of Light, April 2022, https://www.pointsoflight.org/wp-content/uploads/2022/03/Global-Civic-Engagement-Research_US.pdf.

3. "Undivided: Gen Z Purpose Study," Porter Novelli/Cone, 2019, https://www.conecomm.com/research-blog/cone-gen-z-purpose-study.

4. John Mackey and Raj Sisodia, *Conscious Capitalism: Liberating the Heroic Spirit of Business* (Brighton, MA: Harvard Business Review Press, 2014).

5. Charles Duhigg, "What Google Learned From Its Quest to Build the Perfect Team," *New York Times*, February 26, 2016, https://www.nytimes.com/2016/02/28/magazine/what-google-learned-from-its-quest-to-build-the-perfect-team.html.

6. Evan W. Carr, Andrew Reece, Gabriella Rosen Kellerman, and Alexi Robichaux, "The Value of Belonging at Work," *Harvard Business Review*, December 16, 2019, https://hbr.org/2019/12/the-value-of-belonging-at-work.

7. Michael Slepian, "Are Your D&I Efforts Helping Employees Feel Like They Belong?" *Harvard Business Review*, August 19, 2020, https://hbr.org/2020/08/are-your-di-efforts-helping-employees-feel-like-they-belong.

8. Sull et al., "Toxic Culture," *MIT Sloan Management Review*.

9. De Smet et al., "'Great Attrition' or 'Great Attraction'?"

CHAPTER 8: THE TEAM

1. Carol S. Dweck, *The New Psychology of Success* (New York: Random House, 2006).

2. Daniel Sgroi, "Happiness and Productivity: Understanding the Happy-Productive Worker," Social Market Foundation, October 2015, http://smf.co.uk/wp-content/uploads/2015/10/Social-Market-Foundation-Publication-Briefing-CAGE-4-Are-happy-workers-more-productive-281015.pdf.

3. Shawn Achor, *The Happiness Advantage: The Seven Principles of Positive Psychology that Fuel Success and Performance at Work* (New York: Currency, 2010), 130 (ebook).

4. Francesca Gino, "Cracking the Code of Sustained Collaboration," *Harvard Business Review*, November–December 2019, https://hbr.org/2019/11/cracking-the-code-of-sustained-collaboration.

CHAPTER 9: THE INDIVIDUAL

1. Zak, "Neuroscience of Trust," *Harvard Business Review*.

2. Donald Sull and Charles Sull, "10 Things Your Corporate Culture Needs to Get Right," *MIT Sloan Management Review*, September 16, 2021, https://sloanreview.mit.edu/article/10-things-your-corporate-culture-needs-to-get-right/.

3. Workplace Knowledge and Productivity Report," Panopto, accessed June 7, 2022, https://www.panopto.com/resource/valuing-workplace-knowledge/.

4. Dhingra et al., "Help Your Employees Find Purpose," McKinsey.com.

CHAPTER 10: YOUR CULTURE FROM THE OUTSIDE IN

1. Fran Biderman-Gross, "Align Your Brand With Purpose, Inside And Out," *Forbes*, June 1, 2020, https://www.forbes.com/sites/forbesagencycouncil/ 2020/06/01/align-your-brand-with-purpose-inside-and-out/?sh=1ce48cc54eba.

2. Denise Lee Yohn, "Build a Culture to Match Your Brand," *Harvard Business Review*, December 17, 2019, https://hbr.org/2019/12/build-a-culture-to-match-your-brand.

3. "The Experience Equation: How Happy Employees and Customers Accelerate Growth," Forbes Insights in association with Salesforce, 2020, https://forbes. docsend.com/view/32kx5ji4mw5g7dfe.

4. Holly Muscolino, Laura Becker, and Alan Webber, "Relating Employee Experience to Customer Experience," IDC, July 2021.

CHAPTER 11: ESTABLISH BASE CAMP

1. "Return on Culture," Oxford Economics.

About the Authors

JAIME TAETS is a CEO, public speaker, author, podcast host, and thought leader, making her uniquely qualified to address this internal culture crisis. With over twenty years in corporate culture, thirteen of which were spent leading large-scale global transformations, Jaime has honed the craft of bringing leaders and their people together for a unified goal.

As chief vision officer and founder of Keystone Group International, Jaime and her team focus on leadership development, organizational strategy, growth, and change. What drives their work with clients is her belief that strong leadership and a change-resilient culture are the foundation for sustainable growth. Harnessing her experience leading thousands of executives and hundreds of companies on their large growth plans, she inspires real and sometimes challenging discussions about the crossroads between high performance and healthy change.

When Jaime is not writing books or helping leaders and organizations grow, she tries to spend as much time outdoors running, hiking, and being in nature. She lives in the Minneapolis area with her husband and their four children.

CHELSEY PAULSON is the chief strategy officer at Keystone Group International. Her fifteen years of leadership experience in a mid-size, employee-owned technology organization led to her passion in culture development + revival, strategic growth, and leadership growth.

Chelsey built her career being a strategic partner to executive teams, growing the culture, and focusing on strategic people initiatives aligned with the business initiatives such as building trust, internal communications, aligning the right people in the right seats, and succession planning.

Chelsey enjoys serving on multiple boards. She chaired two board of directors where she had the opportunity to coach and mentor the president/CEO of the organizations.

Chelsey lives in the Minneapolis area and loves spending time with her husband and three children at the kids' hockey games. She also enjoys biking, downhill skiing/snowboarding, or watching University of Minnesota sports. When Chelsey is not writing books, using her superpowers to help leaders grow, or with her family, she unwinds by listening to podcasts and audiobooks while running outdoors.

THE CULTURE CLIMB WEBSITE AND TOOLS

What is true of culture is equally true of the ideas, strategies, and tactics to support culture: they will always evolve. The way the Impact Model looks now may not be what it looks like in one year or three years. The tools we created may change as clients' needs change and the conversations around culture mature. We know this, so we have created www.thecultureclimb.com as a place for our community to find information, tools, and support as they embark on their own journey. We hope you visit and share your climb challenges and successes with us.

FIND A CULTURE GUIDE

Embarking on a journey like the Culture Climb is a big decision and it's not always easy to maintain the momentum and focus you intend to. If you need assistance assessing and planning for your Culture Climb, reach out and we can help get you going and keep you moving.

WWW.THECULTURECLIMB.COM

SPEAKING ENGAGEMENTS

Sometimes the best way to create the energy around your Culture Climb is to start with a training or keynote for your team to get them excited about the journey ahead. If you are looking for a culture or leadership speaker for your next event, reach out to us.

WWW.THECULTURECLIMB.COM